Transition

ISBN 13 -978-1542922098

ISBN 10 - 1542922097

Transition

This is my story of surviving an alcoholic home.

The book is a work of non-fiction, based on the life, experiences and recollections of Jo Huey. The views and opinions are that of Jo Huey. The names within the book have been changed to protect identity and privacy.

Jo Huey

This book is dedicated to my Dad, for all his faults I did love him.

"Your life does not get better by chance; it gets better by change."

Jim Rohn

FOREWARD

I first became aware of Jo Huey when she contacted me to ask if she could use some data that I had published on a webpage. From there we started communicating about projects that we were involved in. I had the pleasure of interviewing her for our website for families of problem drinkers, Bottled Up (www.bottled-up.com). She then interviewed me for her website. I have been really impressed by her dedication to helping people and her energy in getting her business started and writing this book. So I was honoured when she asked me to write the foreword for her book.

We all like a good 'survivor' story, stories about people who have faced incredible difficulties and are still here to tell us about them. These stories are inspirational; they show us the resilience of the human spirit, show us a glimpse of what we are capable of, while making us grateful that we don't have to endure those conditions ourselves.

Usually the stories we hear about are beyond our own experience, expeditions to the north or south poles, climbing Everest, single handed sailing round the world. We can picture ourselves in those expeditions, battling against the elements without ever leaving the comfort of our armchairs. It is too easy to believe that survivors are exceptional people who have overcome exceptional circumstances. Yet we are surrounded by survivors: people who have been subjected to prolonged and terrible ordeals. But their voices and stories are rarely heard.

Jo Huey is one of those survivors and this book is her story. It is a raw and, at times, harrowing account of growing up in an alcoholic household. Jo, and so many children of alcoholics, never knew the security of knowing that she was coming home from school to a safe environment. In her household, she might open the door to find the 'nice' dad who was kind, playful and fun or the angry, violent dad who would physically abuse her.

Jo details the unpredictability of her home situation and the effect that it had on her life as a child and later as an adult. She highlights two issues that were directly attributable to her chaotic upbringing. The first was that having been starved of consistent affection, she craved it wherever she could find it.

In dissecting her later relationships, she shows how her craving for affection led her into promiscuity, in the mistaken belief that sex was love. Also, because in her childhood love and affection seemed to have been given so arbitrarily, she was hugely insecure about being lovable. This led her to try to fit into what she believed other people wanted her to be. In trying to be loved, she lost the ability to be who she was and lost the love of herself. But this a book about a survivor and Jo survives; indeed she much more than survives.

This is a book that's squeezed out of painful experience. It's a raw, visceral and highly personal book and is so much more powerful for being that. If you are looking for a literary masterpiece, then find another because this is not it. But if you are looking for a book that might change your life then look no further, this is it!

Few of us can identify with the hardships faced trekking across the Arctic Tundra. Most of us can identify with the struggle to be authentic, the quest for love. Many of you will identify with Jo's experiences of her childhood and her adulthood, although you may not have the insight to realise the connections between childhood situations and adult behaviours. This book helps make those connections explicit.

One of the strengths of this book is the "Insider Tips". Jo relates an incident or a pattern of behaviour and then gives an insider tip which explains the link between the incident and behaviours and some aspect of alcoholism. Using this device, Jo acts as a guide through the mysteries of the alcoholic family.

In the second part of the book Jo leads us through her relationships and in her brutally honest fashion she lays herself bare about failed relationships, promiscuity and even rape. What emerges from this journey is that she is aware that all is not well, as are so many others, but what puts Jo alongside those exceptional people who conquered the arctic is that she is not an armchair explorer. She is willing to seek out and try anything that might help her change, that might help her become a better, more rounded person.

In this book she shows us that she is not afraid to confront what most of us find the scariest creature on the planet – our own self-image. She explores various change techniques: Al-Anon, NLP, retreats, meditation - in this ongoing voyage of self-discovery. There is much to recommend this book but perhaps the most important message of the book is that you can change. Instead of sitting, blaming fate for not giving her a great childhood, or blaming her alcoholic father for disrupting the formative years of her life, she did something about it. She could not change her early life but she took responsibility for her adulthood and how she behaves today. Not for her the bitterness or hate that would have been so easy and even understandable. Just look at the dedication of the book: This book is dedicated to my dad. For all his faults I did love him. This is not just surviving, this is transition.

Jo now has a business making people aware of the problems that alcohol can bring and helping people to recover as she has. If you are looking for a guide for the ultimate adventure then Jo Huey is that guide.

Dr John McMahon.

Bottled Up

Contents

Transition

Prologue

It's Sunday 20th January 2016, and I'm sitting in my aunt and uncle's lounge in Cuffley, Potters Bar. It is a beautiful setting, out of the busy city with lovely views in the garden and infrequent visits from squirrels and birds eating the seeds hanging in the feeders.

Inside the house everyone is relaxing and enjoying the slow pace of a Sunday. My aunt is starting to prepare a lovely roast beef dinner, for which I can't wait. My cousin Josh has just returned from his holiday to Spain with his girlfriend and they are contemplating a walk.

It all sounds so normal doesn't it? But this environment is very different to the one I recall as a child.

If you are reading this book and have lived with an alcoholic, or are a child of an alcoholic, you may not be aware of the characteristics and behaviours that were developed when living in this environment. This book is about my life, what I did to change, and how I came through a destructive home life. Back then I was a defenceless child who was lonely, misunderstood, ignored and scared - but I can honestly say I feel proud of the person I am today. I never thought I would ever say that.

Like many others, I have faced challenge after challenge and got through it all. I have learnt so much and this is what I want to share with others. I want people to understand more about how you *can* cope with difficulties, change what you want to - and learn to accept the things you're unable to change or are happy with.

I will be open and share my innermost feelings about how

tough it was to live with a drunken father that was absent most of my life; and a mother who was scared and intimidated by him. For those reading this with little or no experience of alcoholism, it's important that I explain about the typical environment. Otherwise this book may come across as confusing, inconsistent and contradictory.

When you live with an alcoholic, you can swing from loving them and wanting their approval and affection to hating them and wishing they would disappear. It's like a pendulum - and you can go from one to the other in an instant. You are forever living in hope that things will be different, not wanting to believe that this is the life you have.

You want the person to change but they don't. You can see the part of them that is loving and caring but is controlled by alcohol. So, while there were some extremely horrible things about my Dad and the impact he had on my life; he was still the only Dad I had and I loved him. It wasn't a healthy environment by any stretch of the imagination, but it was the only one I had and the only lifestyle I knew.

I adapted my own behaviours, as I will explain, and I could go from one extreme to another - be close to someone one minute and not the next; trust someone then not.

I will explain the therapy and techniques I learned to help me overcome my traumatic childhood. I want to inspire others to know that there are healthy ways of coping, change and acceptance *is* possible, but most importantly so is forgiveness of ourselves and others. We can be who we want to be and we can deal with the hurt that we felt; we can't remove the memories but we *can* deal with the emotions associated with them. Some people just want to cope with the situations they are in; you will find some helpful and practical tips in this book.

For many years, I didn't show any signs of emotion; because I didn't know how. At home, we were never allowed to talk about our feelings, we had to hide much of what went on – being openly emotional wasn't something I was used to. And I still find it hard to say how I feel - often I just state facts and tend to be logical rather than using words like "when you did that it really hurt me" or "I'm feeling really angry with you."

Insider Tip

In an alcoholic home, you learn to 'Not Feel, Not Trust and Not Talk'. Ignoring the elephant in the room becomes normal, you can't trust the alcoholic because they are so unreliable and lie to get what they want and you keep the family secret because of the shame and embarrassment you feel. Feelings aren't acknowledged because the focus is always on the dramas of the alcoholic and it isn't safe to do so.

Since my childhood and through doing a lot of personal development people often said to me to "Take care of yourself" or "Be kind to yourself" but I never knew what that meant. It sounded good, but on a practical level I had no idea how to do that. I now interpret it to mean that I need to give myself a break; quieten the voices in my head saying negative things; and lower my expectations of myself (you must know the ones I'm talking about?)

3

However, I'm currently in the best place that I've ever been in my life. I feel so much happier in myself, and I'm finally starting to accept who I am. I've successfully increased my confidence and self-esteem, learnt how to set boundaries for myself and how to stop compromising what others want over my own needs. I now have better relationships, more empathy and understanding of others - plus a whole lot more. So, if anything, that should be a great inspiration and motivation to anyone interested in some self-development, learning ways to cope and raising self-awareness!

In March of 2015, I'd already decided to go travelling alone all around America, in which was the biggest step I have ever made in my entire life. This reflects how far I'd come and even now the impact of that journey is becoming more obvious in all I do.

But before I left to go to America, I decided to start up my own business. I attended a course to learn more about being self-employed and what I needed to know about setting things up - once I returned from my travels my intention was to focus on getting my business started because I didn't want to work for someone else any longer.

Sometimes I take a step back and reflect on what I've achieved and I realise I'm finally able to feel pride in my achievements, instead of giving myself a hard time because I haven't achieved enough. Being the child of an alcoholic is tough.

I suppose I should start by explaining more about where it all began.

Chapter 1 – My Family

It's important to take you back to the beginning. So, let's start with my home life, and I'll introduce you to everyone and how life was for me back then. I was born in the summer of 1975, I lived in a semi-detached house with my Mum, dad, older (by four years) sister Daisy and Sandy the golden retriever. The house was painted white with chesterfield green window sills, a long driveway down the left-hand side as you look at the house and right by a main dual carriageway. We had a small garden with a big garage full of food and 2 chest freezers and it also doubled up as my Dad's welding workshop.

I have three older half-brothers, one from my Mum's first marriage and two from my Dad's first marriage, sadly one of my brothers passed away when I was 17 years old but I will talk more about him later in the book. I never lived with any of my brothers so it was mainly my older sister and I.

My home was big inside. As you walked through the front door, which had a small porch, you came into the hallway, on the left-hand side was a door to the lounge which was at the front of the house. It had a few interior décor transformations in my time but it mainly consisted of a u shape sofa, TV and a lot of gifts given to us from the international students that stayed in our house.

From the hallway, the stairs took you upstairs but to the left after the lounge was a large bedroom and then further down the hall we had an under stairs area for coats and one of those old-style dial phones that hung on the wall. Opposite this was a wall covered with a huge map and lots of pins in it to indicate where our students were from, Mum also pinned the different currency around the edge of the map. As well as this were more gifts from the students that stayed with us. This created a very ethnic theme in the house.

The hallway then led into the very large kitchen/diner. Dad did a lot of DIY in the house over the years and he built wooden units on the right which gave Mum lots of space for all her baking things.

We had a small downstairs toilet in the kitchen and beyond the kitchen was my Mum and Dad's bedroom, it was an extension on the back of the house so gave us lots more room.

The kitchen, as with most people, was the hub of the house. We never used the front door, we always came in the back door which was in the kitchen and people would always come and go.

Upstairs we had a small bedroom as you came to the top of the stairs which was the warmest in the house because it had the central heating boiler in it. Next to that room was the bathroom, then from the top of the stairs you would turn back on yourself up a few steps to another bedroom which was mine for a time. Then, at the very front of the house (above the lounge) was the biggest room which at times I shared with Daisy.

It overlooked the dual carriageway, had triple glazing for the noise and was a bright room.

One of the things I reminisce about that room when Daisy and I moved into it was the ceiling. It was as dark as a pair of dark denim jeans. My dad thought the easiest way to cover it was with white foam square tiles so that is what he did, so it went from dark to exceptionally bright. It was all decked out in grey and pink with matching curtains and duvets and we both had a sliding stand-alone wooden wardrobe each. I loved it!

The house wasn't a family home in the traditional sense because our lives revolved around looking after international students. We'd have 4 or 5 at any one time and sometimes more in an emergency. It helped the language schools but we needed the money too. Apart from the family and the students, of course the elephant in the room was always present. We never spoke about my dad's drinking, we just had to adapt and cope with what was to follow.

Life at home was unpredictable but we did manage to have some element of routine in our lives, without that I'm not sure how we would've all coped. Daisy and I went to school, did homework, and played with friends. Mum worked numerous different jobs, dad managed to hold down a long-term job as a welder and we enjoyed the odd social event or outing with Mum.

My Mum was (and still is) an active person, always busy, methodical, organised and motivated - which is probably where I get it from. Her kindness, caring and thoughtful attitude is something I admire. It's important to her to show

7

she cares for people, and for them to know they were important to her. She loved that feeling of helping someone, the satisfaction that something she had done had made a difference to them. She has a big heart and I see a lot of similarities between us now I'm older.

Mum got around on her bike and still cycles everywhere although she has upgraded to an electric one now! She used to take me to school on it; I would sit on the back in a little seat. I recollect wobbling myself left and right in the chair to wobble the bike. It used to drive Mum mad as it made it hard for her to cycle, but it made me laugh so much. She would come and pick me up, never late and always reliable which may sound like a given to most people but in such an inconsistent and unstable environment that I lived in it wasn't to me.

When Mum wasn't looking after everyone in the house, doing chores at home or picking us up from school, she worked. I look back on her having several different jobs to bring the money in; mothers were not just parents even then but employees and more. One of the jobs she had which was my favourite was the local bakery at the top of our road, so not surprisingly Daisy and I loved to go and visit her after school and get ourselves a cake or two. I used to love the Devon splits which were like a bread roll cut vertically down the middle filled with artificial cream and a blob of bright red jam in the middle. Delicious, I still love them to this day but they aren't as easy to find unfortunately.

Mum and Dad met when they were both working at Millers bakery. Before they got together they were both married previously with two children each. Mum had Joe and Daisy with her husband Paul but sadly, Joe and Daisy were split up when they were about three years old - Paul had Joe and Mum had Daisy. Not something that would happen nowadays, but it did then and it had a bad effect on both the children; they wanted to be together as brother and sister but that just wasn't possible and I know it broke my sister's heart to be separated from her brother.

Dad was married with two boys, Jake and Rob. I don't recall how old the boys were when Dad left their Mum but I know he struggled to get access to see them.

My Dad was an interesting and, dare I say it, quirky character. He was a private person who struggled to connect with others; he did have some friends but not many but then that isn't unusual for men. He was a big fan of black and lived in tracksuit bottoms. At times I think he stretched to grey and white but that was the extent of his wardrobe. He liked good quality things and enjoyed listening to music, specifically Foreigner and Elton John. He loved doing DIY and welding in the garage so we had a lot of items made from metal!

The best way to describe him was charismatic, passionate and creative he loved to keep busy just like Mum but also enjoyed relaxing in front of the T.V. Mum and dad were happy together for a few years and he loved and doted on her. He would do anything she needed and he did make her laugh.

Pinpointing the time that Dad started his relationship with alcohol is a hard one and my mum can't remember when or why it all began, but to be honest I don't think there was a particular day or event, it just got progressively worse.

Unfortunately, the alcohol turned my dad into a Jekyll and Hyde character. If he wasn't drinking he would be kind and considerate, helpful, playful and fun. He had a dry sense of humour and used to have us all in stitches. We'd have rare moments like this and I'd grab them with both hands because you never knew when the encounter of the 'nice Dad' was coming.

Insider Tip

In an alcoholic home, you live on eggshells, you never know how the drinker is going to react, what they will say or do so you have to anticipate their every move.

The drinking turned him into a different person, he would shout, and his facial expression would make me shiver in my body. The tone of his voice was enough to make me nervous and sick to the stomach, he was that scary. This was intimidating and meant I was always on hyper-alert - causing me to suffer from anxiety, although I didn't realise it until later.

He was never a big physical presence in my life but I've only just recently become aware of this fact. Of course, I saw him, but I was at school in the day and he worked which isn't unusual; but he never joined us for dinner, I went to bed and he rarely came to say goodnight so we didn't see him until the weekend. He wouldn't join us to watch TV or read us stories at night and rarely came out with us at the weekend.

There was a lot more to come as I grew up but the journey was just beginning for Mum, Daisy and I.

My sister Daisy and I had our moments. We both have different personalities. Growing up she was the 'good' child and I was the 'trouble maker'. She is three and a half years older than me and we had a typical sibling rivalry relationship. I was the one that would question things, ask my Mum "why", whereas Daisy would be the one to just do as she was told. I soon realised Daisy was the 'perfect' daughter in my eyes and I felt left out and misunderstood, because I was different and not easy to understand (from other people's perspective); I thought I was just inquisitive.

Daisy and I had our differences but she was still my sister. We used to play together and amuse ourselves with silly made-up games which I now think showed great creativity and exploration. These days' kids need to have entertainment provided for them or technology to make them happy but we used to find our own fun and spend a lot of time outside. A few of our favourite things were playing on our 'special tree' in Queens Park which we used to climb up and then throw fir cones at each other. We loved it there and had lots of laughs; we use to walk the dog and play around the pond and just have fun with each other and with friends. It was a great escape from the house and we could just do what we wanted, when and how we wanted to do it. It was freedom!

Myself and the neighbour's kids used to play 'block' and I went around to their houses to play computer games and do a bit of baking with their mums. We all got on well and I pretty much lived in their houses, it seemed like a better place to be than home.

There were a lot of good times but for some reason they tend to get over-shadowed by the bad. If I had a bad experience with Dad, Daisy would be there for me and vice versa. We would understand how the other felt and help each other get through the difficulties.

Because we constantly had foreign students staying with us I didn't always have my own bedroom. Daisy and I shared, or I had to share with my parents. I hated not having my own room and often felt like there was no space in the house for me. Our home wasn't our own because it was constantly full of other people. When we did get the house to ourselves we relished each moment.

It was a busy house with people coming and going. The kitchen was the hub, there was a great atmosphere when people came over and Mum's friends would visit. I didn't have a lot of friends over because Dad was quite strict about it. I think this was due to his military training and experience and his need for control. It's also possible that he didn't want people over because he was ashamed of his behaviour and didn't want others seeing his life. Home was his private space, his secret space.

Generally, when Dad wasn't around the house, there was a relaxed feeling and we could have quite a laugh when jobs weren't being done. Mum, Daisy and I would enjoy a lovely Sunday tea with crumpets, jams, salads, ham and nibbles watching the A-Team with the fire blaring out the heat on a cold day and we would all snuggle up and enjoy the moments of relaxation.

My Home

Me climbing up our tree at Queens Park

Chapter 2 – My Mum and Dad

Looking back, Mum did teach me a lot. At the time, I had no interest in chores and being responsible - what kid does? I just wanted to be free, have nothing or no-one to think about and do things for. However, if I hadn't been made to do things to help, and learn those skills I wouldn't know what I do now. I learnt how to cook, bake, clean, save money, entertain myself, sew and make clothes, which in retrospect seems impressive to me. When you are about 8 years old, I don't think you appreciate the value of these things, it's not until now I value what I know and what I can do with it.

One of my favourite times was sitting down with my Mum and watching her as she sat at her Singer sewing machine to start some creation or other. It all started with a visit to the local fabric store. I felt like a kid in a sweet shop with all the pretty fabrics and accessories. Not knowing which way to look, what to pick up first as my eyes darted from one place to the next taking in the massive choice in front of me.

Mum would head to the patterns to find something suitable, I didn't really know how it all worked but she knew exactly what to look for and translated the information to me so I could understand. We'd pick up the pattern and head to get the right fabric as you had to get the right fabric for the item you were going to make, apparently.

After that we picked up the threads and any elastic or other fastenings we needed and headed to the till. Whilst I didn't always know exactly how it would look by seeing it on a roll I was excited to be spending time with my Mum and learning from her. We got home and would get everything out. Mum would take her time and I was impatient with excitement and wanted to get started.

I would help lay out the fabric and attach the pattern all ready for cutting, and then we would start some sewing. The machine was old and had a funny foot pedal but mum would be the one to operate it as I stood at the side watching eagerly. The process seemed to take a lot longer than I had expected and I just wanted it finished. We made a pink A-line skirt for the summer and I was so pleased with it when it was finally done. There were many more sewing projects to come and it certainly was cheaper than buying them from the shop and a lot more fulfilling.

Mum and I didn't have a lot of one to one time but the time we did get I enjoyed, I loved the sewing and as well as that we would bake. Mum loved her sweet treats and I think that's where I get my love of cakes from. We would make Peppermint creams, eclairs, biscuits and butterfly cakes which never seemed to turn out as good as my friend's ones. I couldn't work it out, they were always flat. I loved making lovely treats as much as I loved eating them, the trouble was it would take so long to make some and they would go so quickly.

I won't lie, my relationship with my mother has been very rocky over the years and I feel like I'm finally letting go of a lot of hurt but you should understand that there was a lot of it and just because I became an adult doesn't mean I could easily let it go. Let me explain a little more.

Living in such an unpredictable environment made it necessary for Daisy and me to be independent and know the practical things, because we ended up having to support Mum every day. My Dad was not present in more ways than one. That meant we had to be responsible at an early age and help around the house and do chores.

Mum wasn't the strongest of characters and struggled to stand up to my Dad because he was quite intimidating, I didn't really understand at the time why she wouldn't speak up and felt very let down by her. I needed her to protect me and stand up to my Dad when I wanted to go to a school event or have friends over, but she didn't feel comfortable doing it a lot of the time so we ended up missing out on things.

A lot of the time Mum was very busy managing the house, students, working and raising Daisy and I so time was a limited resource to her. I really felt deprived of attention because Dad wasn't there and Mum was too busy. I understand that she had a lot on her plate but at the time I just wanted her to be available more.

Because of some of the situations that occurred at home I felt that as a parent my Mum was the one to fight my corner as it were, unfortunately this wasn't something she found very easy to do. I'm a strong person and have really struggled to get my head around this. I have a whole lot of expectation and morals about how a parent should behave and treat their children and I guess that is very idealistic and we are all imperfect.

With my feelings of anger, sadness and hurt I punished my Mum for most of my life. I think a lot of these emotions were misdirected at her instead of my Dad. What I never appreciated until very recently was that she too was a victim. When I realised this I cried so hard my tummy hurt, I hadn't cried like that in a long time but I just felt such guilt for being so horrible to her. I will go into more details later in the book as to why I had such strong feelings about my Mum.

Dad used to keep himself to himself a lot, not coming out with the family much or wanting to do the things we did. He ate on his own, sat in his car a lot, or was in the garage welding (by trade he was a welder for a Ministry of Defence company). He felt like an outsider most of the time.

He was a vault of information, feelings and thoughts that rarely opened, which made it difficult to have a relationship with him. I was an optimistic child that hoped for acceptance and attention, which never came. It does sadden me that my Dad was not a big part of my life but I had no control over this.

He had high expectations and standards, most probably from being in the army, although it doesn't matter now, he was who he was. Nothing that Daisy, Mum or I did was ever good enough for him. Now, I realise this was *his* issue, but as a child you want the acceptance and love and attention of your parent. I just wanted him to give me an accepting glance or smile, reassuring words and say how much he loved me, but this never came.

17

Life isn't always easy and we all do the best we can with what we know. I believe deep down my father would never consciously hurt our feelings - he probably thought his strict ways and rules would teach us something. It did, but it also created a fear within me which caused me to hate him most of the time. This was the impact of him having an alcohol addiction.

Fact: Alcohol is classified as a disease

What is a disease? "A disorder of structure or function in a human, animal or plant, especially one that produces specific symptoms or that affects a specific location and is not simply a direct result of physical injury". **Oxford Dictionary**

Not everything about my Dad was doom and gloom and I do believe he was a good, kind and caring person. When he was sober, he would do anything for anyone and enjoyed cars, golf and watching TV. He did have some good points – he loved my Mum to bits and would do anything for her, and he was loyal. He was good at DIY which I know Mum appreciated and would always tackle tasks even if he didn't know exactly what he was doing, seeing it as a challenge. I'm the same, I like to learn and teach myself new things - it makes me feel like I've achieved something.

Our life was up and down, not knowing what was happening from one moment to the other. We were always on heightened alert, never able to relax as we had to be prepared for anything that could happen. We enjoyed the good but were always anticipating that the bad was just around the corner. Generally, if he was off drink then there were quite consistent periods of peace but they were rare.

18

Most of my life I knew Dad as being a drinker. The drink made him one person and he was a completely different man when it wasn't in his life. We didn't have that luxury because the damage had been done; we'd developed character traits that you simply can't change with the click of your fingers.

Mum and Dad were together for twenty years. Today as I write this it is the anniversary of his death – he passed away twenty years ago, two months before my 21st birthday. I like to think that in the main the relationship between my Mum and Dad was good for a long time - but I don't know. I do know that it was difficult for my Mum in the last four years or so of my Dad's life.

Mum is a quiet and shy person and she did whatever she needed to do for a quiet life.

Dad was a tactile person. I recollect him being kissy and cuddly towards my Mum but also that my Mum was embarrassed and not totally comfortable with his outwardly public signs of affection. It's interesting how different people can be, but somehow, they made their relationship work. Or maybe they learnt to compromise and find a way to accept each other as they are. I'm not sure if that was the case, or if my Mum just ignored things for a long time because it was too hard to deal with.

As I got older I saw less and less of the affectionate side of the relationship and more distance, coldness and withdrawal from my Dad. That is a sign of alcoholism (now known as alcohol dependence). Drinkers withdraw because of the shame of their drinking and the only thing that matters is the drink. Everything else takes a back seat and doesn't exist, and unfortunately that's hard when you have other commitments such as children and a job to pay the bills.

Insider Tip:

Money is a big concern in an alcoholic home. The drinker will lie about needing money so they can get what they want – alcohol. Others have to go without, worries about paying the bills arise and arguments start.

I thought, what is the matter with me? Or why doesn't Daddy want to play with me? Or spend time with me? But then it was the same with my Mum too. She was so busy with other things that we didn't often share quality time together. There were expectations on me which were unfair, I recall constantly feeling I wasn't good enough or that I didn't do what my Mum or dad wanted.

My relationship with my Mum and Dad was strained because they both had other distractions, drink for my Dad and running the house and getting the money in for my Mum as well as her addiction to my Dad's alcohol problem. It's not until now I understand the stress my Mum must have been under with money and looking after us, as well as the house and the students. I wanted love, acceptance and support from my parents, but at the time they just were not able to give it, or at least not in the way I wanted it.

Thankfully, I had my sister Daisy with me and whilst we had a volatile relationship we did have some things in common - coping with living in an alcoholic home with an abusive and aggressive father; and for me personally an absent mother.

My Dad

Cleaning my bike

Chapter 3 – My Relationship with Daisy

Being able to confide in Daisy did help me; I didn't feel completely alone which was reassuring. We both experienced Dad's aggression and violence; and we both had to endure hours of his lectures in the kitchen while we stood there and waited for him to finish. We just had to stand up and allow him to say what he needed to - he shouted; then he calmed down, then he shouted and eventually we could leave.

We did talk to each other about it. We discussed a request Dad frequently came up with; he used to say "when are you going to change?" and my response would usually be something like "tomorrow Daddy". Daisy said to me once that she didn't know how he thought we could just change like that; it was like a light bulb going off in my head. After that I use to say to him "I don't know". Reflecting on this, I have realised that he struggled with difference in others. If someone didn't behave how he liked or could accept that was hard for him and he wanted to change them in a way that he could cope with. I certainly relate to this and at times struggle with this myself but over time have become more flexible.

If I didn't do something how he wanted it done (and this applied to my Mum too) then they would think I was being disobedient. But I just had my own way of doing things. I liked using my brain and being creative, and sometimes I just wanted to try things out my way.

They were both controlling - Dad because of his army background and Mum because of the environment we lived in. She had to control things otherwise it could be a disaster.

Insider Tip:

Those living with an alcoholic develop control issues and want to control an uncontrollable environment. This is to minimise the anxiety that living in an unpredictable environment creates. They are afraid that if they aren't in control things will be a lot worse.

Daisy would usually do as she was told, which is a complete contrast to how she is now. We are different in our character and nature and maybe that is why we had so many arguments as children, we hated each other. Although we had to share a room and do things together it wasn't by choice. We had moments of affection but generally we annoyed each other and kept out of each other's way where we could. I know that isn't uncommon with siblings and it's something you tend to grow out of. Thankfully we did.

Daisy was the older, responsible sister; always there for Mum, helping her with what she needed. I preferred to be on my own doing something creative, using my computer or out playing with friends. We both had to do chores and help Mum with the running of the house. We would go with Mum and Dad to Sainsbury's to do the weekly shop, and then to Iceland and any other shop we needed; just to save money. We both helped Mum with the students, much to my annoyance, but Daisy was generally the one who seemed to get it right. I was the one who got told off, rather than Daisy.

My personal belief is that because Daisy was so accommodating and easy in terms of what was wanted, it made life a lot easier for Mum. If you listen to the stories they recall, I made her life a living nightmare! I accept I was probably not the most obedient child but I had my reasons - I just wanted the attention of my parents and I never felt the relationship I had with either of them was that good.

This created an intense and destructive relationship with my parents if I'm honest, I hated being in the house and ran away a few times because I felt so unhappy and unloved. My parents may have loved me in their own way, but it never felt that way to me. There were many contributing factors and it just wasn't a safe and happy home - it felt like a prison at times and that was not the life I wanted for myself.

Dad was always picking on Daisy about her weight and asking her when she was going to lose it - a never ending horror story for her. For me this was just another example of 'you aren't ok' which you don't need or want to hear from your parent. If Dad wasn't picking on Daisy, he was giving me a hard time about the way I was and why wasn't I helping Mum enough.

There's nothing more destroying that your parents saying you are defective, or not making the time for you and showing love and support.

Daisy and I both experienced aggression from my Dad, hitting us around the head, legs or wherever took his fancy. I think the drink had a lot to do with that, but I do wonder where all his anger came from. What was he so cross about, that he had to take his aggression out on his children?

We also both experienced sexual abuse and inappropriate touching from my Dad, I didn't think it was right but I had nothing to compare it to and I certainly didn't talk about it to anyone outside the family. In any case, it made me feel uncomfortable and upset and I did speak to my Mum about it but I didn't feel she did anything to stop it, not that my Dad would've listened.

I chose to face these issues later in life but it took me years. I had to face what happened to me and how it made me feel, and that was one of the hardest things I've had to do. There are still scars and things that trigger me into a state of anxiety but I have better ways of dealing with it now, which I didn't have then.

Nothing Daisy and I said to each other would make a difference in terms of things changing, but it gave us solace to know we were going through it together. We had to be strong and reassuring when the chips were down, our hatred of each other was put aside when things were bad.

We didn't talk to others about what was going on at home simply because it was ingrained in us that we didn't discuss it. We had to live one life with our Mum and Dad and another with friends. This must be hard for people to grasp who weren't privy to this lifestyle (which is a good thing), so I feel I need to explain how this works.

Because everything about alcoholism is about shame, for the drinker and for the family, you learn to not talk about it. I became exceptionally good at compartmentalising my life and adapting to whatever the situation. I could be whatever and whoever I needed to be in any given moment.

25

> **Insider Tip**
>
> **Children of alcoholics become people pleasers and are constantly seeking approval. They are oversensitive to the needs of others, they get their self-esteem from others judgement of them. This in turn means they strive to be perfectionists to be accepted. The better they do, the more positive 'strokes' and feedback they get which makes them feel good.**

If someone needed an understanding friend I was your girl. If a boyfriend wanted a specific type of person, then I could be her. Obviously, this sort of thing can't last but it was what I did and I did it for many, many years. I adapt well to different situations because that is what I'm used to. I adapt to business situations, personal difficulties – I'm excellent in a crisis too.

Learning that 'customising' myself in this way, as I called it, was not the best way to live my life when I got older; but it was only a few years ago that I began to stop doing it. I suspect there are moments where I still say what I think people want to hear, do what people want, just to be accepted, because for me that's what it's all about.

Looking back, I simply wanted to be loved and accepted as me, Jo Huey. You would think that is quite a simple and easy thing, wouldn't you?

Chapter 4 – My Childhood Friends

Growing up I didn't have a lot of friends, I had the neighbours' kids and one or two friends from school but that was about it, I always felt others had a lot more than me. I met a girl at nursery and we went to infant, junior and secondary school together. We still see each other now which is great. I struggled with friends at school not fitting in a lot of the time, and always feeling misunderstood.

Being opinionated is who I am; which doesn't go down well when you have opposing views or are judgmental with others which I learnt from my parents. I wasn't like that all the time but then I seem to have a sketchy memory of my early years.

Thinking about it I spent a lot of time with the neighbours' kids rather than ones from school. We lived nearby so it was convenient, and we all got on so it made it easy. I enjoyed being alone, or out of the house, because at home it was too much hard work or I was uncomfortable. Being with others in their homes was liberating and fun, it was great to laugh and do things we didn't do at home.

> **Insider Tip:**
>
> **Adult children of alcoholics don't really have fun because it's stressful. The child inside is frightened and to appear perfect they tend to exercise strict self-control. Also, having fun isn't an important part of living in the home, it's about surviving.**

For example; I used to love going to Ian's house and helping his Mum do some baking; or to Gemma and Sally's house to watch their Mum make wine with the yellow gorse flowers you find in the parks and forest. She would put on batches of popcorn and I loved the smell of the buttery popcorn kernels popping away in the pan with a waft of the beautiful smell as we lifted the lid to check it was nearly done.

Thinking about my childhood now, I do feel sad but I survived it. Whilst I felt anger, fear and sadness in my home life, I know now that deep down my parents did love me. Learning more about myself over the years has enabled me to understand the situation my Mum and Dad were in; and what possibly caused them to make the decisions that they made for themselves and the family.

I have said those words to myself a lot over the years and sometimes I don't feel grateful. I just don't understand how two parents can allow things in their lives to get so out of control that they affect the lives of their children. I wanted to stand up for myself, tell my Dad how horrible he was being, but he petrified me - I just didn't have the nerve to do it. A child should never be in that situation in the first place. I had no way to deal with the situation I was in. I couldn't physically fight back against my Dad to protect myself; I had no authority to make my own decisions and no knowledge of what was and was not appropriate. I didn't know that my life was any different to other people and I didn't understand what was going on.

Even now I realised how hard it is to 'see the wood for the trees' when you are in any situation. You need the distance between you and it to get a clear perspective. That was not an option for me because I was a child and I didn't know what to do, or who to talk to about it. When I talked to my Mum she didn't seem to take me seriously.

She tried to do what she could but it took a lot for her to muster up the courage to stand up to my Dad for fear of his reaction, and that fear overwhelmed her over and above her duty of care to her children. It also consumed her and stopped her either seeing or admitting there were problems and getting help. There are some parallels here with my Dad, he couldn't see or admit there were problems or get help.

It's the parents' responsibility to keep their children safe from harm, but my home was nothing but a danger zone at times. Not only my Dad but certain of the students made me feel nervous and unsafe. I did what I thought was the only thing I could do, and told my Mum all my worries; however, it seemed to fall on deaf ears. I'd often get that feeling you get when you are talking to someone and they are looking at you, and you are looking at them, but you know 'they don't believe me'.

I believe my Mum and Dad were both in denial for different reasons. My Dad was in denial about his drinking and his general behaviour and what effect that had on his family; and Mum was in denial about both the impact he had on us and

29

how she contributed to it.

My Mum didn't have the skills to teach us certain things because she was never taught them herself. She had learnt to avoid her emotions - as soon as anything painful came along she would distract herself and bury it somewhere deep inside. She wouldn't be conscious of doing this it was just an automatic reaction.

Neither Daisy nor I knew how to cope but I always faced my fears. We are often stronger than we think - it is our stupid overworked brains that tell us otherwise. Dealing with upset is painful but not dealing with it makes life even more difficult in the long run.

There wasn't anything else I could've done as a child to help myself and make myself feel safer. I did what I could with the resources I had at the time - I avoided being in the same room as my Dad, did what I thought he would want to avoid getting hit or into trouble. But of course, it was never enough. My home wasn't safe but that is all I had, and I had to make the best of it.

Insider Tip:

Living as if we are victims is another common behaviour trait, we live our life as if we are and then attract that weakness in our love and friendships. We love to help those we perceive are weaker, to feel useful and to help them so we can get positive feedback and feel better.

Chapter 5 – Interactions

Making the best of my home life wasn't something I found easy. I experienced so much loneliness - who would think that was possible in a house full of people?

I lived a life that was structured and controlled by my parents; Mum because control gave peace and comfort; and Dad because it made him feel powerful. Being an inquisitive child, I was always asking questions. I wanted to know what was going on and why my Dad was like he was.

Daisy and I would do things together when we weren't getting on each other's nerves. One of our favourite things to do was to play 'libraries' as we called it, we would take turns in being the person coming in to rent a book. We would set up our Ladybird books on the floor in the lounge, and have a ticket that would be put inside whichever book we wanted to borrow and the person doing the serving would pretend to stamp the book and give it back and tell the other when it was due back. We loved it and it kept us entertained for hours.

When I spent time with Mum I did enjoy it, when we were baking or sewing I liked to ask how things were made. I didn't like just being told to do something without understanding why; it wasn't a case of being defiant or difficult, it was because I had a hunger to know how the world worked.

Because then maybe I could control it better.

Stimulating my brain and being active was important, I felt like a vacuum wanting to suck up all the information. Unfortunately, my Mum found this frustrating and difficult.

You may have heard of the saying 'children should be seen and not heard', I got the feeling that is what my parents wanted from me. I wasn't like Daisy; she would just do as she was told with no questions. She would never ask why or challenge what people said, they were her elders and she had the utmost respect for them.

It didn't matter to me who I was asking, as far as I could see they were questions, nothing rude - just me needing and wanting to know more. But at that time children had their place and it wasn't for a child to know things that weren't relevant or their business.

It was hard to know how to improve my relationship with my Mum; we are different people and just because we are family doesn't guarantee we will get on. I've heard other people say this and whilst it is hard to hear, it is true. Thankfully, I've managed to realise that how I've been acting towards my Mum is from a place of anger and hurt and learning to let that go and forgive has been a long time coming. Sometimes you just don't like or get on with your family, I know I had periods with Daisy where we just didn't like each other. But we do still love each other.

Dad was forever saying that I would never be able to do the things I dreamed about and I should be 'realistic'; choose options at school that would help me get a job etcetera.

Dad never inspired me or supported me in a way I believe a parent should do. I see now how my friends treat their children and whilst part of me admires it, a big part is jealous and often I feel like they are spoiling their children.

But that isn't the case at all. They are just doing what parents do, taking their kids to clubs, events, parties and school; supporting them with their homework; telling them they can achieve and do whatever they want to. They listen to their troubles, and tell them they don't have to worry about anything.

My life was the opposite of that. I had to get myself everywhere I needed to go, bike or bus. Dad rarely took us anywhere and Mum didn't drive. Dad was absent much of the time; and Mum wasn't academic - she tried, but she wasn't always able to help with homework. At the time I felt my dreams were never encouraged; and I had to face the cold truth that I wouldn't be able to even attempt achieving my dreams or take a risk. Sometimes I came up with random ideas like wanting to be a pop star or something but I didn't want to hear I couldn't do it, that completely shattered my excitement. It didn't matter to me whether it was a practical idea or that it was likely, I just wanted to embrace it and have fun with it.

Mum did listen at times to my troubles but I always felt it was with half an ear out for something else. Her attention never felt like it was 100% on me in any given moment. This is understandable now because she had so much on her plate at home and I do believe she did her best. As for worrying about things, I felt I had the world on my shoulders, and the responsibility that came with living in an alcoholic

33

environment felt too much for me. I spent far too much time worrying about things and feeling on edge, anticipating what was going to happen, if an argument was imminent or if I was going to be shouted at.

One thing I recall vividly is that my home was never a safe place to be, it should be the main place where you feel safe but for me there was danger, a lot of unknowns, and I had little or no way of protecting myself.

Chapter 6 - Fun Outside the Drama

Being in a house full of students for most of my childhood was an interesting experience. At times, I enjoyed having them there, learning about different cultures and of course receiving the gifts they bought us was always very exciting. I would go into their rooms and just chat to them or try to talk if their English wasn't very good. I would help teach them new words and at dinner we use to chat to help them improve their English.

Once a student we had from Switzerland bought us a massive bar of Toblerone, it was so big about 3 feet. The slices were massive and we had to chop it up with a big kitchen knife.

As I grew up and started to understand more about the home I was living in and what was going on around me, I spent a lot of time on my own. I use to sit in my bedroom when I had one and listen to Radio 1 and record the Top 40 charts on my audio cassette, stopping and starting it when the adverts came on or a song that I didn't like. It was fun but a little time consuming as it went on for a couple of hours. I used to nip out of the room and miss the start of a song that I wanted to record or forget to turn the tape off and end up with lots of adverts.

It was something my friends did too and my sister. It was just one of those things, a way to get the music you wanted to

35

listen to without having to buy different albums from the shop. I didn't have a vinyl player but Daisy did and when we were sharing a room she used to play her records which weren't my choice but I started to get into some of them. Some of my favourites were Genesis, Tracy Chapman and Eurythmics. I bought some vinyls to use on her machine and played them all the time, my music choice was not as cultured as Daisy's.

Kylie Minogue, Bananarama and Whitney Houston were my favourites. I would sing along to them in the bedroom all the time. Daisy use to like me singing to her and one song in particular was her favourite, It was 'Love Shack' by the 'B-52's'. I used to sing it and animate myself at the same time and it really made her laugh.

Sometimes I would do creative things at home, making cards out of whatever odds and sods we had. I enjoyed drawing as well, not that I was any good at it but I liked to use the colours and sometimes do patterns and colour them in. Drawing outside the lines wasn't something I let myself do and it was still very controlled. I do remember painting out in the garden with Daisy on a beautiful summers day. Mum would put aprons on us to make sure we didn't get paint all over us, good idea I thought. Then she would get creative herself and find a clothes airer than was like an 'A' shape. Daisy would stand on one side and me on the other and Mum would attach the paper with some pegs and we would stand there like Monet and paint our masterpieces.

We'd check each other's painting out and have some fun whilst we were doing it, the sun would be beating down on us and all the stresses of our home life just melted away for a few hours.

On the weekends, sometimes we would meet up with Mum's friends, Jean and Philip were her friends from school and they had two children Sara and Eva. Eva was nearer Daisy's age and Sara nearer mine. We would visit their house in the next town and us kids would play together whilst Mum and Jean chatted. Dad would come along I think or sometimes just drop us off. I don't remember a lot I just know that we saw them every now and then.

We didn't really have many family holidays, we just couldn't afford it. I would wish that we could go abroad like my friends at school did, but it never happened as a family. When I was about 14 years old and Daisy was about 18 we had the opportunity of going to Turkey to visit our student Hakken. He lived in Istanbul and it was somewhere Dad had previously visited and I was keen to go and have my first holiday abroad.

Mum managed to get everything arranged and save up the money for our flights, Hakken said he would have us at his house and his girlfriend would be there with us in the day whilst he was at work.

Daisy and I were both really excited for this opportunity, we flew from London and I remember vividly being in my seat next to Daisy as the plane left the tarmac and was on an incline as it pulled away, I turned and said to her "Is it going to be like this the whole way?", she burst out laughing and told me no it would straighten up once we were high enough. I felt a sigh of relief because it didn't make my tummy feel good and I thought we wouldn't be able to walk about.

We only went there for a week and it was plenty long enough. We stayed at Hakken's apartment and had our own room. It was plain but fine for us both, with a window to the left and the double bed just as you came in the room on the right.

We must have arrived on a Saturday because Hakken wasn't working, and we spent some time with him down the beach from where he lived. We swam in the Black Sea, Hakken was all ready for his swim and walked us down to the water edge where there was a wooden walkway out to the water and he did this high dive off the edge and into the water. I thought, that seemed cool I'll do the same. Well image this, a 14-year-old girl diving off the edge deep into the water only to discover it wasn't very deep at all.

What went wrong, my perception of the depth was totally masked by Hakken's amazing dive and it wasn't until I hit my private parts on the sea bed I realised I'd underestimated the depth. I shouted to Daisy "I've just whacked my f**** on the bottom", she fell about in hysterics. It was so painful, I didn't try that stunt again.

It was so warm in the water, not at all like home. Daisy and I are such water babies so we were entertained for hours. We headed back to Hakken's after a great day out with him, and his girlfriend made us a lovely dinner. One of the days we were there Hakken's girlfriend took us to see him at work, it was a big corporate building and he had a massive office. I couldn't believe the size of it but then everything seems big when you are little.

One of the days when we had time on our own we took a

walk around the local area, we met these Turkish guys and they took a keen interest in us. I felt very apprehensive but was OK because Daisy was with me but I was very cautious. They got far too familiar with us too quickly and I started to feel uncomfortable, I was only 14 so not that old. They were a lot older than me and kept hassling us.

They convinced us to go with them, I went along with what Daisy did and they took us to their house and tried to get us to kiss them and have sex with them which I wasn't going to do. They wanted us to watch pornographic movies and I was so scared. I couldn't believe we went away for a nice holiday only to find ourselves in this potentially dangerous situation.

We got out of there as quickly as we could and headed back to the flat, I felt terrified that they would follow us and know where we lived. They were pushy and wouldn't take no for an answer so we had to be quick and just leave. Thankfully we made it back safely but this has really affected my feelings around dating foreigners.

Hakken's girlfriend started off being nice to us but as the week went on it became obvious that she didn't want us there. We entertained ourselves most of the time and took ourselves out for the day. I think I was quite lippy to her and she didn't like me so would not give us dinner and things like that to punish us.

One evening she had friends round and basically told us to stay in our room so Daisy and I played a lot of cards and just entertained ourselves. She really was mean and it upset me but we were in a foreign country and Daisy reminded me we had to do as she said.

That night we went to sleep and I remember it so well, there we were in the land of zzz and suddenly I was woken up abruptly, Daisy had a cat on her leg. It happened faster than I can explain it but she basically screamed and then swung her leg to the right where the window was to fling the cat out of it. I was shocked but at the same time I was in fits of laughter, it was so funny one minute seeing this random cat on our bed, on her leg then the next minute it must have wondered what was happening as it flew out the window.

We laughed for ages and I think Hakken's girlfriend told us to shut up but we couldn't help it, we still laugh about it now.

One of the days nearer the end of the holiday we went out for a walk and found a hotel with an outdoor pool. We relaxed there and had a swim but neither of us had much money left so we could only buy a bit of lunch and a drink and had to share.

When the end of the week came, we were grateful to be going home because Hakken's girlfriend made it very difficult for us to feel at home there. It was a pity as this could have been great fun but she really dampened our experience. It was lovely to see Mum and Dad again and fill them in on our trip and what happened, we didn't really keep in touch with them after that holiday which was a shame because I think Hakken was really controlled by his girlfriend, he was so sweet and nice.

Other than that holiday we never went abroad with Mum and Dad. We had some holidays in Devon which I enjoyed, but it wasn't often. We usually just stayed at home and did day trips out to places like the beach and things local to us. There was an amazing place called 'Tucktonia' and I remember my uncle taking Daisy and I there. It isn't there anymore unfortunately but it was such fun.

We went on these bikes and the handlebars were going in the opposite direction than they were meant to, so to go left we had to turn right. It was tricky and I fell off a few times. It was an adventure wonderland with lots to see and do and it was nice to spend time with my uncle. He was married to Becky at the time and they would spoil us when they took us out. We didn't get to see them often as he worked away in South Africa in the casinos but when he was home he would visit and take us out.

Becky and Uncle Mitch took us to a toy shop once and basically said have whatever you want, a child's dream! I choose a plastic toy washing machine and Daisy choose a Chicaboo which is a type of teddy bear but they were really popular in the 80's. If you Google it, you'll see the images.

We would also go around their flat when they came back to the UK and I remember Daisy and I trying on the fur coat that Becky had in her wardrobe and my Uncle took some polaroid's of us in them. The coat was as big as we were. We also had some of Becky's high heel shoes on so with those and the brown fur coat we looked very grown up.

Daisy reminds me that I slept a lot when I was young, I wonder if it's because of the anxiety and stress of the house but I don't know. I just know I was tired a lot. When I woke up I could be in a bad mood which wasn't great for everyone in the house.

When I needed to get out for some time on my own, I use to head to the local amusements and spend lots of money on the slot machines. I didn't have a lot of my own money so I would steal the 50p's from the electric meter cupboard. We had to put 50p's in for electric which is odd now but that is how it worked back then. With the money in my pocket I got on my bike and cycled to Sea Road where my nearest amusements were.

My favourite game was a card game called Hi-Lo. You had a card and then had to guess whether the next one would be higher or lower, a bit like Bruce Forsyth's TV show. I loved it and I loved winning, I got really addicted to it. I would always tell myself that is the last time, no more, but it got the better of me and I just kept playing. Eventually my Mum cottoned on to the fact I was taking the money and I got told off as you would expect. I still played but only when I had my own money, it never lasted very long and I wouldn't usually come out with much if anything but I loved the buzz of it.

Insider Tip:

Those affected by someone else's drinking often develop their own addictions. This fulfils our abandonment needs.

Time to Reflect

Reflecting on my home life makes me see how complex it was, however when you are living in the environment and so close to it that is hard to see.

It's only recently that I can see how things aren't as straight forward as I saw things when I was a child. People don't purposely choose to do the wrong thing in the main, they do what they do because they believe its right or maybe they can't do what's best because of their own limitations.

Not understanding why my father drank is something I will never know, I can't imagine he would have purposely chosen to behave in the way he did and make the choices he did for no reason but for him that was hugely affected by the alcohol.

Different personalities clash too, Daisy and I are quite different and I wasn't smart enough or old enough at the time to know any better, to understand how to form better relationships. I wonder what it would've been like had we've been closer.

Mum and I were also at odds but that was each of our ways of expressing ourselves, we muddled through but it was like wadding through treacle at times. The house could be at times a fun place to be but sadly I seem to remember all the bad stuff and not much of the good.

Not fully appreciating the efforts my Mum went to, to provide for Daisy and I was something that escaped me. I

43

concentrated on what was wrong rather than what was right, a negative outlook. I do feel sad for my Dad because I think he must have been terribly lonely and totally disconnected from his feelings and being the person we all feared and disliked a lot of the time couldn't have been nice.

Chapter 7 – The Abuse, Alcohol and Fear

It's important to explain more about the worst part of my life at home. Although what has gone before in this book has all contributed towards my mental ill-health both as a child and subsequently as an adult; what I believe severely affected me was the inappropriate behaviour of not only my parents but others living in our home.

For some people this will be hard to read but it's the truth, and it's from my perspective of what happened in my life. For years, we had to keep things secret, not make a fuss, minimise things if you will. I still probably do that - but this is important, and it's time I shared it. Alcohol is a powerful drug; the effects are widespread. Each drinker is affected in different ways.

> *Fact: If alcohol was re-classed today it would be a class A drug*

My Dad began acting strange when I was 5 years old, so it would've been 1980. There are specific events and actions that happened, but others escape me and probably for good reason. I learnt that when I was growing up my 'Daddy' would like to look at me physically, he would ask me to take my clothes off to see how I was developing and would touch me. I felt scared and uncomfortable, literally frozen to the spot but my mind was 100 miles away.

Being so young I didn't understand how inappropriate this was. He was my father and I trusted him. I convinced myself he was checking my development. I was at his mercy and had little control of the situation so was confused with what to do. I wanted to run but I knew he would stop me or hit me, I didn't want to stay but what choice did I have? I was fixed to the spot and resistant to do anything, I felt embarrassed and unbelievably uncomfortable standing naked in a room of strangers just looking at me. I was the focus of his attention and I didn't like it one bit.

Looking for my Mum to come in at the right moment, to witness what was happening and save me from this horrendous encounter with my father never seemed to happen. He seemed to time these things well, but thankfully eventually I escaped. Often that is what I wanted to do, just escape from the situation, people in the house and at times the house itself. That's why I was so angry towards my Mum.

At other times, I had to experience sleeping in the same room as my Mum and Dad; it felt like there was never room in the house for me. This fed my sense of worthlessness.

Insider Tip:

Those living in this environment develop a sense of low self-esteem. This is affected by the need to be a perfectionist so you don't attract criticism. There is no way to meet the unattainable standards of perfection we have internalised from childhood and we are always falling short of the expectations we have set. If we are responsible for a positive outcome we will minimalise it by saying "oh that was easy". So, we rarely feel good about ourselves.

Wanting my own space to feel safe was something I longed for and seemed like a luxury. I didn't enjoy having to sleep in my parents' room with Daisy as well, it was a squeeze and not having any personal space made things very difficult and uncomfortable.

One day, Dad locked Daisy and me in the lounge when Mum was out and made us watch an adult film. I'd never seen anything like that before and I felt so embarrassed and scared. Thankfully Daisy was with me but I didn't want to look at the screen. Dad kept telling us to watch it and for us to see what was going on. We complied with his request because it wasn't safe to do anything else. It's disturbing now to think of this; and to even begin to understand what was going on in my Dad's head. He just wasn't thinking with a sane mind and his behaviour mirrored that. Thankfully my Mum came to our rescue and banged on the door; she got a key and freed us. At least she was there to protect us from Dad's strange behaviour.

That's how it felt; set free from this torture that my Dad put us through, though I don't think he thought he was doing anything wrong. That experience has affected me. These incidents do impact us in the long term.

Much of the time we had a house full of foreign students, so having my own room was a luxury not a right. I walked in on one of the students when he was having sex with his girlfriend. I just ran away and told my Mum. I didn't know where to look or what to do, I literally just shut the door and left. Feeling embarrassed and confused as I couldn't understand why the door wasn't opening, we use to go into the students rooms all the time.

47

Another time, one of our Arab students asked me what the word for a body part was, pointing to his penis. I was so petrified, I just ran downstairs and told my Mum but I don't recall her saying or doing anything. I don't think she believed me, so what signals was that sending to me? I had to learn to fight my own battles. It wasn't my Mum's fault I guess, she hated confrontation and this was someone helping to pay the bills and we needed the money.

Home was not just unsafe it was scary, especially when Dad was drinking heavily. He was sectioned a couple of times to St Anne's, the local psychiatric hospital. Mum said he was in a padded room, but I can't recall much about it, I just know it happened. He was admitted to hospital on a few occasions due to drinking – He was yellow, yellow! which Mum explained later as jaundice.

Dad was just not a well man and the urge to drink was just so great he couldn't be a proper father. He would be manipulative and tell all sorts of stories and lies but think we didn't know. I probably didn't so much at the time but knew things weren't right.

Insider Tip

Drinkers will do whatever they can to pull the wool over your eyes, lie and cheat and tell you what they think you want to hear. Everything should be taken with a pinch of salt.

He would hide drink everywhere, and Mum would find bottles all over the place. He would pass out and forget doing or saying hurtful things. He would say sorry a lot and try and make up for things, but when it wasn't received well he would get angry. We couldn't pretend it was all OK when it wasn't. So then the arguments would start, it was a vicious circle.

One day I was at home with Dad and Mum was out somewhere. He asked me to come under the stairs where we had our phone, one of those old dial ones which was wall mounted. He said "Can you see them?". "See what?" I said. He said "Can you see the babies in your school PE bag? I was scared, confused; and didn't know what was happening - why was my Dad saying there were children in my PE bag? I said there was nothing there but he was absolutely convinced and couldn't understand that I couldn't see what he was seeing, it was so frightening. I didn't want to lie but I could see him getting more and more annoyed.

Things got so bad at one stage Mum decided to pack Daisy and me off to my Nan and Grandad's so we could have some time away. We left through the kitchen and walked out the back door up the drive. Dad was walking towards us saying "Who are these children? I thought, "It's me, Dad, Joanne. Why doesn't he know who we are, what is going on?" I had so many questions and not many answers coming my way.

We spent time with my Nan and Grandad but it wasn't the same as home, we didn't have many of our things with us and my grandparents were a lot older and quite strict. That said, my Grandad was great fun but my Nan a little more serious. I did love spending time in the garden as my Grandad had a greenhouse and he use to show me what he was growing which were usually tomatoes and green beans. We fed the fish that were swimming carefree in the pond and tidied up the garden, he use to give us little jobs to do. The boundaries between the gardens were only divided by wire fences so it was open with the neighbours. It was so peaceful and not at all like home.

He also had a garage where he kept his car and tools and bits and bobs. He had this game called Shove Ha'penny where you put a Ha'penny on the wooden board and shove it up the board and the one to get it the furthest won or something like that. I loved it because it was different and I'd never seen anything like it before. There was a certain simplicity to it all at my grandparents, I liked that.

We use to walk in the local forest which I enjoyed as it gave us time to explore and have fun. It was lovely and bright and feeling the heat of the sun on my face as I walked through the trees and investigated every nook and cranny. I did love tea time as my Nan and Grandad had a fold up table we use to cram around and a serving hatch to the kitchen which amused me. I felt like we were in a shop being served by someone. It was just different; an old person feel to it as it were. They had lovely pastel colour small knives and pretty plates which I loved. After tea we'd watch a film on their old style chunky TV. They had a really strange machine with large disks that we used to watch films on, I don't think it was a very popular thing because I've never known anyone else have one.

After a while we went home, dad had been into hospital again to get better but not by choice, by the time we returned things were a little calmer. The constant turmoil in our family was shocking and we had no idea how to get out of it, solve it or help my Dad. He never wanted to go to

Alcoholics Anonymous; sometimes he would stop drinking but then it started again. He was a sick person and no one could help him but himself, he was the only one that could decide to stop and he chose not to. Drink was his life and that was that, we were just the bystanders, the victims in his sad story.

Insider Tip

A lot of people that live with an alcoholic want to help them, there are only a few things you can really do. One is to say how you feel, how their behaviour has changed due to the alcohol and do so with kindness and love. Nothing will stop them from drinking, especially if they feel judged.

My Grandad and I in the garden

My Nan and Grandad

Time to Reflect

There are a lot of years and times that I can't remember, Daisy has a fantastic memory but mine isn't so great. I feel great sadness about the relationship I did and didn't have with both my father and mother.

Clearly, they both had a lot to deal with and their past had affected them to such a degree it meant they weren't able to provide certain aspects to us, their children.

My Mum's first husband was quite a strong character and I know she felt intimated by him. She has since shared stories about her mother and father and how they didn't teach her much. She found out about women's personal health from her first husband and was understandably naive with life.

She did tell me about a time when she was working in a hairdresser and her boss was just standing there watching her, she explained how intimated she felt and when she recollects the story I can see there is still a lot of emotion there.

Dad's parents were apparently quite religious which could be why he was so anti-religion with us. We never met them but from a few snippets of information I gleaned over the years my Dad didn't get on with them. They were quite strict from what I understand, maybe that is where he got it from.

I'm not sure what my Nan and Grandad thought of the whole situation at home, I've never asked my Mum but I know they never really liked my Dad. I don't recall them ever being friendly and chatty to him, he would always have to come with us because my grandparents lived in West Moors which was about a 20 minute or so journey from our house. Hoping that Dad would find his way and stop drinking certainly wasn't on the cards in the long term, or even short-term.

Chapter 8 – Moving Out and Moving On

It was around 1991-1992 when I was 16 nearly 17 years old that my Dad thought it would be a good idea to chuck me out of the house. In a weird way, I think he thought he was doing a good thing. He probably thought he was teaching me some life lessons, and that I needed to get out there in the big wide world and know what it was like. I think this was a period of his life when he was sober which was rare, so I can't even blame the drink for his actions.

For me this was one of the most unloving and uncaring acts my Dad did and there were a lot of them to choose from. Thinking about it now I wonder if it was a good thing because at least that way I didn't have to live in the house that was so unhealthy and I had the freedom to do what I wanted, when I wanted to do it.

That said, it was one of the scariest moments, because I had no income. I was a student, and only worked part-time in a local hotel as a waitress. I spoke to Daisy and she agreed that she would move out with me so we could share a room in a local house. If it wasn't for her I'm not sure how I would've coped. As we got older we started to get on better so it wasn't the worse option for me.

At the time, I felt so angry towards my mother for not standing up to my Dad. I couldn't make sense of it at all. It's only years later that I have a better understanding and more compassion. He really was a scary person and after all my Mum's negative experiences she really struggled to go against what Dad wanted. She was feeling the same as we were I suppose, fearful of his reaction so took the road of least resistance.

Insider Tip:

Mum's reaction isn't unusual to those dealing with an alcoholic. Those faced with an alcoholic become frightened of angry people and any personal criticism. They seek approval so any criticism threatens this which in turn damages their self-esteem.

I'm not a parent so I don't fully appreciate it all but I would hope that if I had children I would find the strength from somewhere to protect them but I think it's probably easier said than done.

In any case, it happened and Daisy and I were living together - I think I felt a massive sense of relief. Daisy tells me that I spent a lot of time with my boyfriend who worked at the same hotel; so, she was on her own quite a bit, which I feel bad about now. She gave up a lot for me and then I abandoned her.

At the time, I think it was exciting having an older boyfriend called Jack. He was extremely good looking and unfortunately for me all the other girls thought that too and he knew it!

In 1992 my half-brother Jake suddenly passed away. It was

unexpected and the whole family were in total shock.

My Mum and Daisy had gone to the beach with Jake's wife Catherine and her children, Julie and Ollie. We used to love going to the beach and would always go to the same place at Boscombe Pier.

I wasn't with them that day, and all I recall being told was that Jake had been in an accident. I was told that he'd been moving some track on the railway where he worked and the tool he used slipped and hit him in the jugular and he died instantly.

At that time, I didn't know my other half-brother Rob and his family. He was also working on the railway that day and was with Jake at the time. I can't even begin to imagine what that was like, being there when your brother had been tragically killed in an accident.

There was a lot of family controversy around Jake's death, as my Dad hadn't been involved in Rob and Jake's lives for a long time, and felt like an outsider when it came to funeral arrangements and dealing with all the details.

My Dad wasn't able to see his sons when they were growing up, but as time went on and Jake got older he started to have a relationship with him. I do recall that we would see Jake and his family occasionally for Sunday lunch. Catherine and the kids would stay with Mum, Daisy and I and the boys would be off doing something together in the garage or tinkering away on something Dad was working on.

They were so similar and they both got on so well, it saddens me that I never had a chance to know him that well and that I wasn't old enough to appreciate him as a person. I also feel upset that I didn't know Rob my other brother and his family; it wasn't until my own father's funeral that we started talking and we still stay in touch.

Obviously, the death of a son was a massive blow to my Dad, and he didn't cope with it well. He said "Why didn't they take me?", and it breaks my heart thinking about it. The immense pain and hurt he must have been in was hard to witness, he loved his sons very much and now one had been taken from him in a freak accident. He cried so much and was inconsolable.

My father was broken and didn't know what to do. He was angry of course because the railway should have provided the appropriate equipment to do the job. There was an enquiry into Jake's death but they found it was 'death by mis-adventure'.

Unfortunately, there were a lot of arguments with Jake's wife Catherine and the funeral arrangements. My Dad wanted Jake's surname to be the same as his on the gravestone but Catherine had other ideas and it ended up being a double barrel compromise. This was all due to Dad being absent from his life for so long, Jake and Rob both had a step-father to raise them, so they used their step-fathers name as well as their natural father's.

This crushed my Dad as he wanted his family name to be carried on, which I can understand.

Jake and his son Ollie

Jake and Catherine's Wedding Day

There were cuttings from the local paper about Jake's death, and Dad kept them all. Sadly, our relationship with Catherine and the children broke down after this and we no longer shared weekends together with the children which was a real shame.

Catherine died several years later from cancer after remarrying and having another child, who later died. The children, Julie and Ollie, were therefore orphans in a sense from a young age and the trauma they have been through is not something I would wish on anyone. I'm so sad that things have ended this way.

With the exceptional and overwhelming pain and hurt that this traumatic event caused everyone, especially my Dad, the demons of alcohol got to him once again.

Insider Tip:

When people give up alcohol after being addicted for several years this is known as them being 'sober' or 'abstinent' from alcohol. This can be the case for years but that doesn't mean they won't return to it. People that are alcohol dependant will always be that and they can never touch alcohol again.

Chapter 9 – Escape

Mum would take us all out to places like Queens Park, Poole Park and day-trips to the Isle of Wight. The beach was a place where we spent a lot of time. It was like a second home. We used to have a beach hut so we had somewhere to put all our things. We would head down there on a sunny day with the heat beating down on us as we walked down the zig zag to the promenade.

Having the beach hut meant we didn't have to carry so much each time so that was a blessing, we just took our own food and clothes for the day. Daisy and I enjoyed having fun playing in the sea, the water could be so clear at times with the tide out so you could walk for ages before reaching the water. It was lovely soft sand and few stones which is very different to how it is now.

We used to also build cars in the sand, Mum was the expert and would come down with us to get the shape of it right. We had seats in the front and back of course but no steering wheel and we made use of the stones and shells for decoration. We were entertained for hours, swapping who was driving and pretending we were chauffeurs to each other. We had a supply of water to pat down the sand so it would stick together but the deeper down we dug the wetter the sand got.

When we were doing that, we were in and out of the sea, playing with our inflatable boat, Daisy would pretend she was taking me on a tour and pull the boat along and give a running commentary of places we were passing and just making it up as she went. We would swap and I would do the same for her. Sometimes we turned the boat over and pretended we were surfing, it was so funny trying to keep upright and make sure we didn't fall off when the waves came in. We would stand there singing "Born in the USA, I'm Born in the U S AAAAAA", they were fun times.

Lunchtimes were my favourite part of the day; we would have hotdogs and burgers which were delicious, dripping with ketchup and a bit of sand mixed in too sometimes. It was like a retreat, a getaway for us and I'm so grateful to my Mum for taking us there.

It took Mum a long time to realise that Dad was no good for her, or the family. Daisy and I had to tell her Dad was drinking again, when you are so close to something it is hard to see the wood for the trees. Eventually Mum plucked up the courage and asked him for a divorce. She said that she hadn't loved him for some time, which is understandable. Living with an alcoholic that spends all your money, who is aggressive and irresponsible doesn't make for a good relationship.

> **Insider Tip:**
>
> **Money in an alcoholic home becomes a big issue because the drinker tends to spend it on the alcohol. Cash reserved for bills and other necessities ends up going missing or getting spent. This causes further stress and pressure in the home and concern for the non-drinker. Lies are told and the alcoholic becomes very manipulative. They can be exceptionally creative and convincing and the cash isn't always used for what they say it is.**

He lied to her and us and intimidated her so she felt she couldn't do anything without his say so. Because of her character, she was too scared to challenge him and what he said went. But his time had come and he had to leave the house - not an easy task. Mum struggled to get him out for quite some time.

It was a relief and massive weight off my shoulders. I had freedom and a chance to breathe. I felt safe in my own home. Thankfully Mum stopped hosting students after a while so our house was our own.

Things didn't just get easier right away, just because Dad left. Times were still difficult for us all. He was drinking heavily at this stage so nothing she said seemed to matter much. There were times when he would listen and do as she asked, but a lot of the time he didn't. He found it hard to accept what was happening and obviously, it wasn't his choice to leave.

He tried to persuade Mum to take him back, time and time again, but Mum was at the point of no return, which was a long time coming.

> **Insider Tip:**
>
> Drinkers take a lot of risks, nothing matters more to them than the drink. They will put that over and above their love of family, safety and themselves. They lose any sense of self-care and when and how they will get the next drink is a priority. They will manipulate situations to get what they want and the drink makes them act exceptionally selfishly.

It must have got to a point where we felt we had no choice. Daisy called the police to tell them Dad was drunk driving. The police arrested him and he was banned from driving but that wasn't going to stop him.

I found out after his death, that despite the ban he bought another car and started driving again. The risks he took and how he treated his children were inappropriate beyond words.

Nothing had changed, just his physical location. He was still the same drunk Dad we all knew and ironically still loved. We cared for him because we knew the drink was a drug that he couldn't resist.

Now I know more about alcoholism I can see so many unhealthy and maladaptive behaviours in all of us.

My friend and I at the beach in our car

Time to Reflect

From 1991 to 1993 there was a lot of trauma going on in our lives, not only the death of Jake but Mum and Dad's divorce, me having to move out and Dad's drinking got a lot worse.

This is a significant amount to have to deal with for anyone in a relatively short space of time and I think it's fascinating to know that it's something my Mum, Daisy and I survived. Sometimes we are stronger than we realise. It's only recently that I have realised that we probably faced Post Traumatic Stress Disorder (PTSD) because of what happened but back then labels weren't as common as they are now.

At the time, it was very unsettling and a lot to cope with and very much a daily struggle, but when you reflect you can see how you were able to get through the tough times and survive it. I think that is testament to how resilient we have become.

Having family to support you through the difficult times is exactly what you need and whilst everyone can be in a different place with it mentally, you do all have similar things in common which you can relate to.

Understanding and expressing emotions can be very difficult and often those emotions are shown in an angry way, a retaliating and hurtful way because if you don't know how to healthily express your feelings then you do it the only way you know how. Sometimes you can withdraw because it's easier that way. Not facing things helps you think that it'll go away and you won't need to face it.

The difficulties we all faced were dealt with in a practical way and we did talk to each other about what was happening, but I don't think any of us knew how to say "I'm really confused, hurt or angry", we just didn't know how to do that. It would have been a sign of weakness so in the absence of feelings we just 'got on with it', acted and carried on regardless.

Chapter 10 - Jack

In the time Daisy and I lived together I was studying college on a course called Hospitality, Leisure and Reception Studies. It was a two-year course which I started in 1991 and finished in 1993. I did it alongside my part time waitressing job at the Moat House Hotel. Daisy was working at The Moat House as a chef and had done since leaving school. Mum also did a bit of casual waitressing like me to get some extra cash so all three of us worked in the same place.

Around this time, I was with my boyfriend Jack. He was three years older than me and at 16 going on 17 that was quite a lot; most of my friends went out with guys their own age. Jack was very good-looking. When I first saw him, I was working at the hotel as a banqueting waitress and he worked in the restaurant. We crossed paths in the kitchen, how romantic!

We got together after a night out at a local club, The Academy. It is an old building with high ceilings and lots of character. As you walk through the front door it has a long wide hallway, and to the right is the cloakroom and toilets. Then from the hallway you enter the main area, and as you walk through the double doors you enter a large space with two levels. Directly in front is a large dance floor area with the stage ahead of that. You can walk round both sides and on the right, was the bar which took up the whole side of one of the walls. From the dance floor there were stairs on each side which started on the dance floor and took you up to the next level.

There was another bar area upstairs and seating all around the sides like an old theatre so you could look down on the dance floor. I preferred it upstairs and the music was more my kind of thing, disco and R & B.

Jack and I went there for the usual dancing and drinking and after a while he took my hand and walked off down some stairwell in the club. I wasn't sure what was happening but I was intrigued to find out, we started kissing. He started to try and have sex with me there and then, but someone came along so we had to leave. I was secretly relieved; I didn't feel comfortable at all. I was still too young to be taking risks like that and it tapped into my anxiety, not that I knew that was what it was at the time. We left the club and went back to my sister's place where I was staying over for the night. One thing led to another and we ended up having sex. It was strange to me as I had no idea what I was doing and he was super confident. I do recall feeling nervous because my sister could have come back at any time so I couldn't fully relax and her friend lived in the room next door so I was worried that she would say something to her but he left before she got back.

I walked home the next day over the bridge near my house thinking I could take on the world, I'd had sex, and I kept repeating it to myself. It felt like a big achievement.

After that we started going out together. He lived in the building next door to the hotel, which was a staff house. I was still naive at that stage and had no idea what I was letting myself in for. He was someone I could escape to, someone who showed me affection and love, or so I thought. I spent a lot of time at his place rather than being in the room with Daisy, I just enjoyed having his company and it was all very exciting.

My lasting memories of the relationship are varied but more than anything I remember it being stressful. There are so many incidents that happened over the period of our two-year relationship.

I experienced him high on drugs, heavily affected by alcohol, sleeping with other girls and I walked in on one of them which I found most distressing. I recall the day so clearly; I was working at the hotel and I had this gut instinct that something wasn't right. I snuck off from waitressing at the hotel at a suitable opportunity and walked over to the staff house, it was the longest walk and my stomach was turning over and over like a washing machine.

I entered the building and walked slowly but apprehensively up the stairs. I approached the door and whilst I had no idea what I was going to be faced with I was still anxious about what was going on behind it. I pushed the door open to see Jack and his housemate from next door in bed together. It was a moment I can't take back and I felt so awkward walking in to this situation, I didn't know where to look, what to do or say. I called her a bitch and said "how can you do this to me?" to Jack and promptly left the room.

Jack didn't even get up and run out of the room after me to try and salvage the situation, I was so upset and couldn't get out quick enough. This was just one in a long line of incidents that I put myself through. I did allow myself to be mis-treated and that is just it, people can't treat you badly unless you let them.

He had an addictive personality and went from one thing to another, he was never able to keep to one person and commit to it. We split up and got back together a few times, he was unfaithful and didn't treat me well at all. Whilst at the time it felt nice to have the affection, there were far too many signs that it wasn't a healthy relationship for me.

Not realising it at the time because we don't do we? It isn't until we are out of a situation we can truly see it for what it is. Isn't it always easier for everyone else to see things objectively because they aren't emotionally attached and isn't it so difficult when you see someone in a less than ideal situation but they can't tear themselves away?

Insider Tip:

It is not uncommon for those already affected/living with an alcoholic to either become one (stats say 1 in 4) or have a relationship with one. It is what they know and they are addicted to saving the person.

The relationship just made me feel bad a lot of the time but mixed in with my need to be loved and have attention I buried it and tried to think that he didn't mean what he did, he loved me really. I was so gullible and spent a lot of time feeling hurt, he hurt me. I talked to friends about it, they questioned why I stayed and I often wondered. I lived in this unrealistic world of hope, hope can be so damaging. It's just a way of not facing the reality and accepting what is.

Accepting what is really happening then means you have to do something about it or decide that the situation is the way it is and won't change. Sometimes I think we all prefer to live in the denial so we don't have to face the truth. I certainly did for a long time and it wasn't going to be the last time either.

One of the times when Jack and I split up I started seeing a guy I met at a club, it was quite a new thing but we got on well. I would go and stay at his place and we would do some cycling together and just enjoy each other's company. On one occasion, we went down to the beach and we were having a nice time and some of the group from the hotel I waitressed at came down and so we all had a catch up and just enjoyed the rays.

Sometime after Jack turned up and it had been a little while since I had seen him, he joined the group and I did feel a bit awkward with both guys being there but I got on with it. Jack said he had something for me back at the hotel so for whatever reason I decided to go, I think deep down I still missed him and so I made my excuses to everyone and left. I did feel bad as it must have come across awful to this guy I was seeing but not bad enough as I left him there.

Jack and I chatted on the way back and by the time we got to the hotel staff house I was feeling a little bit apprehensive as I wasn't sure what he was up to. We walked into his room and I was taken by surprise when he started to grab me and I resisted saying I was with someone else and he couldn't just turn up and expect me to go back out with him or whatever it was he wanted.

In a split-second I found myself face down on his mattress on the floor and he was forcing himself onto me from behind. I shouted and told him to get off me but he wouldn't, he wouldn't listen, he wouldn't stop. I clung to the bed and tried to push myself away but he held me down, I felt myself filling up with tears as they trickled down my cheeks. I was so scared. I couldn't believe he was doing this to me, making me have sex with him when I didn't want to.

Switching off I just lay there and kept thinking I was making something out of nothing and he was my ex-boyfriend so it wasn't rape. I waited for him to finish before I pulled away and told him he was a f**king arsehole and how dare he do that. I scrambled out of there as quickly as I could. I didn't tell anyone about it at the time and it wasn't until years later I shared this with Daisy.

Most of the relationship was a sham and I never should've stayed with him for the length of time that I did but I was vulnerable and had little to no self-esteem. When you lack care for yourself you can put yourself into dangerous situations, I gave my power away to others and always felt they were right or had the upper hand.

Insider Tip:

Adult Children of Alcoholics suffer with low self-esteem. This is connected to the person judging themselves and trying to be perfectionists. This is to demonstrate control so they avoid any criticism which will impact their already low sense of self.

By the time I finished college we were coming to the end of

our relationship. Things were not easy and I slowly came to realise that he wasn't the nicest person I could've chosen.

Living with a father that had an addiction led to me picking a guy that was similar, this wasn't a conscious choice but one that felt right at the time. This was probably the beginning of a pattern in terms of the people I would pick as partners, and the reasons I chose them were to fulfil a need in me to save them, to feel useful and to make them love me because I was what they needed, or so I thought.

Chapter 11 – College, Friends and Fun

My relationship with Jack happened whilst I was at college. I was constantly distracted and consumed with worry about the relationship not to mention all the other things going on in my life at the time, moving out of home, Jake's death and my Mum and Dad's divorced. Thankfully, when I started college, I met Sammy the girl who is now my best friend, she was there to listen.

My other friend from school, Emmy, also attended the same course I was on, so I generally stuck around with Sammy and Emmy.

We used to spend a lot of time in a pub called Little Peters which was across the road from the college where all the students used to hang out. It was fun and a great contrast to my home life so I did my best to enjoy it.

We had similar classes and used to meet up at lunch and have a laugh about our teachers. Sammy and I would take the mickey out of one of our lecturers – Patrick, he was Irish and such fun. The course was easy, we had a mix of practical and theoretical lessons, and restaurant studies was my favourite. We learnt how to carve a duck which we did in front of the customers, we made crêpe suzette which is just posh for pancakes and had to flambé them at the table. We all took it in turns to run the restaurant and we all had an opportunity to work behind the bar and learn about wine and cocktails. I didn't much like housekeeping classes as we had to make beds and learn how to use those floor cleaners which I always visualised someone starting up and getting dragged off down the hallway with as they could get out of control if you didn't hold onto them.

The course was easy and classes were a bit sketchy in terms of a schedule so we had a lot of time off and being students we made the most of it and would nip into town for some girly shopping or just hang out together.

Sammy and I have been friends now for over 24 years, and I have known Emmy for a little longer as we both went to school together.

Sammy is different from a lot of my friends; she was fun in an eccentric way as well as kind and understanding. She is a Christian and her faith is important to her. I didn't understand this about her back then. As my Dad was anti-religious so I probably didn't show much of an interest in it, which I feel bad about now but I just wasn't open to things I didn't understand or like.

With Sammy, I spent a lot of time going to concerts, meeting up and doing girly things together which were fun. Emmy would come along sometimes but I tended to meet them both separately. Emmy and I would go to the Academy and enjoy club nights (which Sammy was not into). One night Emmy and I cycled to the Academy night club when I realised I was going to be late home; I was still living at home at this point.

Knowing Dad wouldn't be happy I let down my tyres intending to pretend I had a puncture. When I got in my Dad was there waiting for me. He didn't believe my tyre story so I had to stand there and get berated by him yet again about not meeting his expectations and standards. He got so angry at me for not coming in at the time he said, I just felt so trapped. I was 16 years old and I was so restricted by his rules with no sense of freedom and fun allowed. It was suffocating.

It's great that our friendship has lasted so long and I hope it continues; sometimes friends are just the medicine you need when you are feeling low or need a boost.

My college friends and I

Sammy and I at home at one of our house parties

From the age of 18, when I left college, I started going clubbing more with Emmy; but also, my friend Melanie who also went to school and worked in the restaurant at the same hotel as me.

We would get ready in the toilets at work after our shift, it was like a movie stars' dressing room with lights around the mirrors and makeup, brushes and loose powder all over the place. With the smell of sweet perfume mixed with deodorant sifting through the air. We were workers entering the bathroom and the party girls were the ones leaving, it was a great transformation. We left the hotel and headed into town for drinks, often we started in a place called the 'Artful Dodger' and went to some other bars before finally ending our night in The Cage and The Zoo, two cool clubs. Melanie drove a red Escort convertible of which I was envious. It seemed so cool. We would cruise into town with the top down thinking we were something!

We did the club scene for a good few years - it was a good laugh. It was also a time when I was promiscuous; I would meet guys at the club and go back to their house, or somewhere else, and have sex. Because sex was such a big part of my life at home and I was exposed to it so often, I didn't feel that this was unusual.

Of course, I used sex as a way of getting the attention I didn't get when I was younger. I felt these guys liked me - they showed me affection and I felt special and worth something. But thinking back now I took a lot of risks, and didn't look after myself. I slept with so many guys but it never made me feel that great afterwards.

It is sad to think those were the choices I made but I did, I would walk home after the night before feeling dirty and cheap, I would ignore the feelings and convince myself it was fun and it really boosted my confidence. I didn't care about them and they didn't care about me, it all just served a purpose at the time.

One night I went out for a night with Emmy and we went to the local nightclub in town. The music was good, and drinks were flowing, and we starting chatting to some guys. Emmy's guy was Carl who she is still with now - and I met Matt. We swapped numbers and after a night of dancing and drinking we headed home.

That was the start of a five-year relationship with Matt - he was lovely, funny, attractive and intelligent. We dated regularly and would enjoy lots of different things. He lived a bit further away but it wasn't far and he spent a lot of time coming back to where I was to see me.

We'd go out for dinner and to the movies together, he'd come back to Mum's as I was living back there after Dad moved out and we would enjoy time at home just chilling out and being in each other's company. It was nice to have someone I got on so well with.

Time to Reflect

My friendships didn't come easy, ever since starting secondary school I found it hard to get on with the other girls. So finally, when I got to college and was a bit older it was nice to meet people that liked me and wanted to spend time with me. I was very grateful to have them there to support me in my times of need.

Sammy reminded me recently of a time when she bought me lunch when I was living with Daisy, she said I was so hungry because I didn't have any money and that I chucked the food down my neck faster than you could say boo. I don't remember this at all but I know I didn't have a lot of money because I was always lending it to Jack and obviously, I had to pay for rent, bills and food from the money I earnt at the hotel.

My Mum did help me out with food and sometimes I ate at the hotel when I was working, Daisy was also working so she could help out too financially.

It was nice to finally have fun with my friends at college and whilst living away from home was tough, I did enjoy the freedom it gave me to do what I wanted without having to answer to anyone which I had to do at home.

Thinking about it I did go from one unsafe and dysfunctional relationship at home to one with Jack. He wasn't in a good place in his life and constantly doing drugs, abusing sex and anything else he could to excess wasn't a good influence on me. My ability to choose people that were like Dad was finely tuned and at that stage I wasn't aware enough of myself and I had a long long way to go until I would get to that point.

Having boundaries, self-respect, self-esteem and self-worth were not on my radar and I had no idea what any of it was. I only wished it had come sooner but then I wouldn't know what I know now and I wouldn't have learnt a lot about surviving in life without it. Thankfully I finally met Matt who cared about me and life was a lot simpler.

D-Day

I was working at a company in Poole and I can visualise the day clearly. It was 2nd May 1996 and I had a call from reception that the police were here to see me. Immediately I thought it was something to do with my Dad.

I went downstairs to an office that was empty and they said "I'm afraid to say that your father has passed away". I was in shock although part of me had known it was about him, I just thought he had done something wrong. I was in total shock; even though he wasn't a healthy man I didn't expect him to simply die. I felt like I watched their mouths tell me the news but my head couldn't take it in fully, I was talking and walking and functioning but I wasn't there. I wasn't with it at all, I was like a machine. I just did what I thought I had to do and didn't stop to take it in.

The police had tried to get hold of my Mum but she was working and I was the next on the list. I went to my manager and asked to leave. They sat me down in the Managing Director's office and asked if I was OK to drive. I said I was because I just wanted to leave.

> **Insider Tip:**
>
> **Those affected by someone else's drinking are exceptionally good in a crisis as that is what they are used to and it gives them a feeling of power and control. The smaller mishaps and changes cause more distress.**

After leaving work I went to find Daisy. I told her what had happened and we had a good cry together. We then drove to the Hotel where my Mum was. On the journey we just talked about dad and the situation, questioning the details and how he was found and what was going to happen. We had a lot of questions and at the time no idea if we would know the truth.

We stood in the hotel kitchen at work and hugged each other and cried. It was all so overwhelming and I didn't know what to do or how to feel. I wasn't use to feelings, for so long we were taught not to feel which is typical in an alcoholic home, you don't feel, don't talk and don't trust. All I ever did was react to situations, feelings didn't come into it. I never considered myself I just looked at the situation, reacted and dealt with whatever it was that needed fixing or solving.

> **Insider Tip:**
>
> **It's common for those affected by a drinker to bury their feelings, children in that environment aren't encouraged to share how they feel. They end up fearing all emotions, good and bad.**

But after the initial shock I went into organising mode which was my way of coping. I know Daisy felt I should've waited to sort things out, that it was disrespectful not to; and to be

84

honest she was right. But I just did what I thought I had to do and got on with things; I suppose you could describe me as being a bit like a machine.

We had to arrange the funeral and deal with all the financial details and ownership of his property (which wasn't worth much). We spoke to the people who discovered his body - he was found in the bedsit he was living in, apparently with his head in his hands.

Later, I found out that he had been vomiting blood but he hadn't said anything to anyone. I felt it was such a tragedy, both how my father lived his life and how it ended, slumped in a chair after drinking himself to death.

We told Rob about Dad's death. It must have been a shock to lose his brother and his father within a few years of each other. He did come over to the house and we chatted about Dad and his life and how it was for us. We explained our side of things and tried to understand more about his life and why we never saw him and his family.

It was such an eye-opener, for years we only knew what Dad had told us and it wasn't all true and we had this impression and story about Rob that wasn't measuring up when I spoke to him face to face.

The day of the funeral wasn't easy. The hearse pulled away from the kerb with the funeral director walking in front for a short while. Matt sat next to me in the car with Daisy and Mum. It was an odd experience; it was nice to have Matt there supporting me and knowing I had someone to rely on. I looked out of the window as the rest of the world got on with their day to day lives, it felt like everything should stop, my father had just died for god's sake but it carried on regardless. I was torn in my own feelings because whilst I had a lot of anger towards my father I still loved him and thought I shouldn't be allowed to feel upset because I didn't like him very much. It was confusing and conflicting, very similar to that of my home life.

Daisy and I had planned to say a few words. When we arrived at the crematorium the place was packed; people were standing because all the seats were taken. I never realised my father had so many friends or maybe they were Mum's friends and there to support her.

At the ceremony, we played Elton John tracks, one of which was 'Father and Son' one of his favourites and related to Jake; he loved Foreigner so we included that too. He had left no will so we just did what we thought he would like. I believe he would have been happy with the send-off we gave him and a lot of people came to show their respects.

When it was my turn to step up and say my bit, Matt came with me. I began to say how whilst life was difficult he was still my father and I loved him a lot and that I'd miss him, it got too much for me and I ended up in tears and couldn't carry on. Matt stepped in and finished it for me; as well as reading Daisy's tribute.

It was a lot harder than I thought. People knew I had hated my Dad at times, but he was still my father and I felt loyalty and love towards him no matter what he did. That day was very painful, and the days to follow too. But we all went through the usual stages of grief, until we got to a point where it all became a lot easier, which took time.

We remembered some of the good stuff but unfortunately there was a lot of bad. I didn't want to look back at him that way and for a long time I regularly went to the crematorium to lay flowers where we had a plaque. It was a peaceful space and it allowed me time to think of him, the good part of who he was. I loved being there and it gave me the time and space to just be, to reflect and consider my life with my Dad and allow myself to feel sadness, anger or whatever arose that day.

I felt loyalty to my Dad but at the same time I hated what he had done and how he hadn't been there for me. And now, he never would. I felt a relief at his passing and felt like a fraud grieving and being the one people felt sorry for. These two things conflicted with my hatred for my dad and this caused me a lot of confusion. How can I hate him so much and yet cry at his death? It didn't feel right to be relieved that he had gone. I kept feeling I was a bad person for feeling that way. I couldn't understand my feelings and that was because we had been taught not to have any. I had Daisy to speak to about it. She understood.

I spent a lot of time worrying about what everyone else was thinking. People who came to the funeral, people who knew about my Dad's death. Were they trying to take advantage of his money? Did they feel sorry for us? Did they like him? My anxiety peaked at that time and overthinking things was a big problem for me. I always had to be prepared for what might happen at home.

> **Insider Tip:**
>
> **The unknown is not something children of alcoholics feel comfortable with. They control their environment as best they can so they are prepared for any scenario. It can be extremely exhausting.**

It is sad because I should have been able to grieve like anyone would in normal circumstances but my circumstances weren't normal. I hadn't realised it back then but I had developed (and still have) OCD certainly when it comes to organising. That is why I went straight into organising mode when we found out Dad was dead.

My actions upset me now. It seems disrespectful, but it was my way of coping. Having to get things in order because my life had been so 'out of order'.

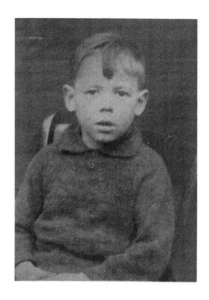

Dad

Dad with his football team mates

Time to Reflect

The death of my father came as a great shock to me and everyone else in the family. Although we all knew he was ill we just weren't expecting it at all.

There were so many mixed feelings at the time and it was very confusing. I wish I had known him better, had the ability and maturity to help me but deep down I know I couldn't have. I would have loved to have had more time with him as an adult but unfortunately it wasn't meant to be.

He has missed so much of my life and the rest of the family. Knowing what I know now about alcohol I'm surprised we all survived it but I think you just find ways to live in the chaos. I do feel sorry for my Dad because he clearly couldn't talk about his feelings, open-up and tell people that he was hurting or that things in his life weren't great.

He went through a lot of issues himself and the death of his son was a huge emotional trauma for him to cope with and his way of dealing with life was through alcohol. Back then the help was there but not like it is today, he wasn't interested and we certainly had no idea we could have had help for ourselves.

We thought the issues were his and not ours, he was the one that needed the help. If we had been able to go to Al-Anon or at least be open to speaking about things, then it would have been a different result but as it was we didn't take that road and we all turned to our own ways of coping.

The pain Dad put us all through was very difficult but I suspect it was no more difficult than the pain he felt himself. The torture, guilt and shame he had to deal with because of his actions and choices. I missed him then and I miss him now and I hope that he is in a better place.

Chapter 12 – Time of change

After a time, we all moved on but Dad's death lingered in our lives. Of course there were times of upset and times I missed him and the person I hoped he was or that I saw on the rare occasion came to mind. As the months went on it got a bit easier.

Not long after Dad's death in 1996 Matt and I bought our first house, daunting but so exciting. I was still working at the same company but left about a year and a half after Dad passed away.

Once I left my job I had about three months of unemployment which was the first time in my career. I managed to find another job which was based in another factory in a small village. I ran the office and booked in orders and dealt with any issues that the staff had as well as some finance areas. It was a nice little job and the people were friendly, it was interesting being in an engineering environment again and not something I sought out but seemed to happen.

The company got taken over whilst I was working there and it took some time for everyone to adjust, they had other premises and there was talk of people being made redundant and the offices and factories merging. Eventually the new owners did what people feared and merged the two, I moved to the new premises and they let go some staff and some chose to leave. It was a tough time and not everyone got on, I was having some challenges at work, I don't think I was particularly mature and so my reactions to change and things not going the way I wanted caused issues. I got on well with the accountant although he was quite strict, it was a small office and we enjoyed a joke here and there and made the best of the situation.

During the time I was working at the factory Matt and I spent the first few years of the relationship doing up the house and getting to know more about each other. Living with someone is so different to just dating them. You start to notice the little things that they do that annoy you or the things they do differently to you. It's about compromise and knowing you can't have it all your own way. That wasn't something I liked but something I had to learn over the years.

Working at the new factory wasn't really working for me, the owner's son was quite difficult and I would go as far to say a bully. One of the office girls left because of him and he seemed to favour one of the other ladies in the office. Working there became difficult because I felt like everything I did was wrong. Systems and processes changed so often I would forget which way we were doing things. I didn't get on with the girl that ran the office and we had a few incidents, she was just evil to me and on a power trip as far as I could tell. I remember being in tears on many occasions.

One day I ended up in the boardroom with her and the boss's son and he basically said it wasn't working and let me go. It was a relief and the best thing that could have happened, I wasn't happy and I didn't like how I felt when I worked there.

Whilst I was working at the factory Mum and Daisy moved out of my childhood home. It was 1998 and time for a new start. Daisy had left her job as a chef and her and Mum had set up business together running a local café which was only over the bridge from where we lived. It was on the main road and the place had a canopy that came out from the building with the front door in the middle of the shop. As you walked in they had the counter straight ahead of you and then behind that was an archway to the preparation area that led to the kitchen area and a door out the back to the public toilet.

There were seats in the bay window and then tables and chairs placed around the space so they could get as many people in as possible. I think it could probably seat around 20 maximum.

The kitchen was tiny and I've no idea how Daisy managed, I know things did get tense between Mum and her at times as they worked very differently. Mum would move things that Daisy had left and Daisy would shout at her and tell her to leave it where it was. I think with it being a small space they just got under each other's feet, but they did well. People loved their home-made stews, cakes and breakfasts.

At the weekend, I used to love going in there for a club sandwich or breakfast with Matt when we were off. It was quite a busy café but Mum and Daisy didn't really have much business knowledge and they were selling things far too cheaply to make much profit, but they enjoyed it and loved the banter with their customers.

Daisy had bought her first flat not far away so she had some of her own space. I use to go and stay with her sometimes when we had a night out, it was a nice flat. As you walked in you had a long galley kitchen on the left and then a massive lounge with high ceilings then back towards the front door there was a hallway to the bathroom and then back towards the door was Daisy's bedroom which was a nice size. I remember it as being a bit of a haven for us all to go to when we needed time away.

After leaving my previous job in 1999, I started a new job working for an insurance company which was near to our new house. I was part of their IT department based on a farm, which was quite odd. It was a small team of three progressing to five as the company grew. I worked there as office support for six years and then progressed to IT Trainer for a year and a half.

When Matt and I bought the house, it seemed a little bit out of the way, having never lived in a different area before it took some adjusting. Neither Mum nor Daisy drove, so they had to get the train when they came to visit us. This was awkward, but they did visit occasionally.

Chapter 13 – Unknown Territory

After a while I had a new network of friends in New Milton as most of mine were based in Bournemouth and I didn't see them as much. I met a girl who worked in the local hairdressers. She was sweet and we just clicked. I think you know the moment you meet someone if you are going to get on! I also became friends with one of Matt's friend's girlfriends. They had moved to a local village, not too far from our house. We would meet up occasionally for dinner at each other's houses and do the usual socialising at pubs.

Everything seemed fine. Life was filled with lovely comforting routine, with me usually swimming at the local pool three times a week, working and socialising with friends. Matt worked hard and was based at an oil refinery - he was committed to achieving promotion and getting recognised for his hard work.

We had a lot of fun in the first few years doing up the house - me spending far too much money whilst Matt was working hard to earn it. I used shopping as a way of distracting myself from dealing with life, it was an addiction that I'd developed. It took me out of the humdrum of life and was my escape, I found solace in making myself feel and look nice on the outside so no-one would notice and think that things on the inside were a car crash.

Having decided from a relatively young age that I didn't want children, I felt that I couldn't bring someone into the world that might have been like me. I felt I was broken and that the child would end up with all my negative characteristics. I didn't want that for another human being. I also knew kids were hard work and whilst I'm good with kids and love babies I didn't want to share the attention with anyone else. I know that sounds selfish, but I had a life where I felt I wasn't getting the attention I needed, I didn't want to have a baby that would take my partner's or anyone else's attention from me. Matt and I agreed that parenthood wasn't something we wanted.

We enjoyed some fantastic holidays together, mainly to America. We did a couple of coach trips to places like New York, Palm Springs, Las Vegas, San Francisco, New England and lots more. We loved it and we have great memories from those trips.

We had some nice trips in the UK too and I remember going down to Weymouth for a weekend. We had been discussing getting married and I was a little torn because I wondered what difference it would make to us, but the idea of the dress and everything that went with the wedding day attracted me and I got caught up in it.

Matt had booked a hotel for us to stay in and we had a reservation at a lovely restaurant overlooking the water, it was pretty. During the day we had a walk around the town and did a bit of shopping, it was a lovely day. That night we were getting ready to go out for dinner and Matt proposed to me in the hotel room. I remember it so clearly and I feel so bad about it now but I said "You can't do it here, you have to do it in the restaurant". Talk about controlling, the poor guy couldn't propose without me needing to say how and where and when. It totally ruined the moment and he quite rightly got annoyed and said to forget it.

After the mishap, we went out to dinner and it was a lovely meal, he did propose later that evening and I did say "Yes". We didn't make any immediate plans to get married it was just left for the time being as we weren't in any rush. I was extremely excited and shared my exciting news with my friends and family on our return from our weekend.

Things were going well in my relationship but my friendships started to get rocky. I wasn't getting on with a few of them, and various arguments kept popping up here and there. It got to the point where I thought I needed some help if I was going to keep any friendships I had. I needed to do something or I was going to alienate everyone. Thankfully my friendship with Sammy was still going strong and she moved into a house with her husband just down the road from me, it was nice to have her near so I wasn't so alone.

Sadly, this wasn't the case with other friends and two specific events triggered what I did next but I will explain to you what happened, and why it was important for me to do something or risk losing everything (as I saw it).

One of the events took its toll. My friend was due to get married and had arranged a hen party in Dublin. I was apprehensive because I didn't know anyone, but I went because I wanted to go to Dublin and it was Kim's hen party. I wanted to support her.

From the beginning, the whole event was a disaster. A lot of her friends knew each other and I didn't have the same connection. We all got picked up in a limousine which started from the hairdressing salon she worked at Matt dropped me off and I joined the girls in the car. Immediately I felt a bit awkward because back then I found it even more difficult than I do now to be with a big group of people I don't know, I felt intimated I suppose, not that I realised that was how I felt at the time. I just knew I didn't want to be there.

We made our way to the local airport and boarded the plane after enjoying a drink at the bar. The flight was quick and once we landed we headed to the hotel that we were staying in.

The environment felt strained to me and I had a disagreement with my friend's sister; she was getting quite nasty towards me - I retaliated, and it got very awkward. People weren't talking to me. I was on my own a lot and by the time we got home she had uninvited me to the wedding. It was one of the most humiliating things that ever happened to me and I still have bad feelings about it now. I felt very hurt and I do feel sorry for my friend and that it ruined her hen party.

That was my problem you see, my intentions were always good but I didn't deliver things well, and could come across in the wrong way. Others reacted to that which is fair enough - I didn't mean to upset them but I accept it had happened and that I had to deal with the fallout.

After everything that happened, in 2000 I decided to start seeing a counsellor. This was a decision that was way overdue and it wasn't just the event with my friend, it was an accumulation of disagreements with friends and family over the years. The couple of events were just the trigger that kicked it all off for me. I went to my counsellor on a regular basis for a few months initially. We talked about the current situation in my relationships, and my struggles, and as the months went on we delved deeper into my childhood and the contention with my Mum and Dad.

At these sessions, I learnt a lot about something called 'Transactional Analysis' and being the 'Persecutor', 'Rescuer' and 'Victim', I found the sessions extremely useful and they gave me the support I needed at that time.

I discussed my father's death, the anger towards him and my mother, and all sorts of deep rooted trauma. This decision to seek help was a big one; and the start of big changes for me. Nothing happened overnight, but it started to get the ball rolling and I began to understand a little more about myself.

Time to Reflect

I'm not sure if the death of my father was a trigger for me looking at myself and wanting to be different or whether it was the incidents with friends that I'd been experiencing but it was certainly a very difficult few years for me.

Feeling very misunderstood and probably not understanding myself, who I was or what I wanted, I think had I known that, things would have been very different. I was still very immature in my thinking in some situations but in others I was the most responsible person around and very adult like.

The interactions with my friends in the main was good but I think because it was something I struggled with since senior school I knew I needed to do something to change and I think the situation was forced by the events that happened.

At the time, I thought I was good at expressing my emotions but I can see now that wasn't the case at all. Focusing on others and telling them what they were doing wrong seemed to be where I focused most of my time. It wasn't until I started to seek counselling help that I began my journey of awareness.

Relying on others to make me feel good, look after me and take care of me was something I assumed for a long time. It isn't anyone else's job to do that but I wasn't giving it to myself so I needed it from others. I'm always there for my friends and very loyal and I give my time generously but sometimes I expect the same back and it's not always possible.

My behaviour was very like my Dad's in that I struggled to accept difference in others, if they behaved in a way I didn't approve of or, like or could handle I would turn it around and make it about them when it was about me. My discomfort was who they were as a person, I found it difficult to accept them for who they were.

Chapter 14 – The Break Up and New Beginnings

Things at home with Matt were getting strained. I think cracks had been showing over the years but I persevered. I was lonely and I used to go out on my own without him. We started drifting apart. We both loved and cared for each other but we couldn't seem to find a way through the relationship problems. I started to feel like there was little point in the relationship continuing.

Insider Tip:

Adult children of alcoholics will do anything to save a relationship, rather than face the pain of abandonment which they fear.

Although we were engaged there was no sign of a wedding. We were just coasting through life and not on the same page anymore. My job was very stable which was a blessing, having too much going on at once is too much to handle. I was at the point of ending the relationship. One day my sister Daisy offered me a trip to Dublin with her for a short weekend because it was a friend's wedding. So, I thought why not.

I didn't know anyone but Daisy also took her friend Louise because the guy getting married was someone Daisy and

Louise met when they were travelling in Thailand and India.

When we arrived, we checked into our 'Fawlty Towers' of a hotel with sloping floors, broken windows, dirty bathrooms and a general tired appearance; but it was cheap and in the centre so we stuck it out. We wandered around the main Temple Bar area and did a bit of shopping; and in the evening, we met up with the groom-to-be, and his friends at a local bar.

Two guys walked in, they were friends of Daisy's. I was blown away by one of them and we got chatting. I could sit and listen to his Irish accent all day and night (which is basically what happened!), his name was David.

We had a few drinks in the bar and chatted for ages, we got on well and he was hilarious. After everyone arrived we went to a local club, we walked down the road arm in arm together which was so nice. I thought he was lovely. I still had Matt in my head but he wasn't someone I wanted to think about anymore. I was in Dublin, and I was going to have a great time.

We all had fun dancing and drinking. In the early hours Daisy and Louise went back to the hotel; I stood outside chatting for a while with David. We knew we would see each other at the wedding the next day, so I went back to the hotel to get some much-needed sleep.

My heart was pumping and I was feeling so excited, you know what it is like when you meet someone and there is an instant attraction. I couldn't sleep although I knew I needed to, as it was only a few hours before we had to get up for the wedding. I think I must have woken Daisy up and chatted about David; intrigued if he liked me and all the usual worries girls have - would he call, would he talk to me at the wedding or was it just fun for the night?

The next morning, we all got ourselves ready for the big day. We made our way over to where the groom was at his mum's and enjoyed some pre-wedding drinks. I was excited and nervous to see if David was there, what he would look like, and if we would get a chance to talk.

When I walked in and saw David there, I felt a pang of excitement and nervousness at once; but we chatted about our night out the day before, enjoyed a drink and then it was time to head to the church. I felt apprehensive and wasn't sure what he was thinking but was just pleased to see him again.

We had an amazing time and I spent most of it with David. He was the funniest guy I think I had ever met; and to this day is still the funniest person I know. He had mannerisms just like me and an honest and carefree attitude to life which I loved.

After the wedding reception, we went back to the hotel where we were all staying; David and I walked back on our own. I'm not sure exactly what happened but I was quite drunk, and slipped off the curb and ended up hurting my ankle. I could hardly walk, so he had to help me hobble back in one piece, barely. It was probably a good thing that I couldn't feel it.

It was only in the morning that we realised the true extent of the damage to my foot. It was swollen and I couldn't walk.

David had to head back to his house so we said our goodbyes as we had to get the flight home that day. It was so hard to leave him, we connected over the weekend and when I meet someone that I have that sort of connection with I want to be with them all the time.

We headed to the airport and Daisy had to help me with my bags and walking because I was in agony. The flight was short so that was good but as soon as we got back I went to A & E. I found out I had torn the ligaments in my foot. I just cried. I think I was overwhelmed with emotion from the weekend and knowing my relationship was in turmoil. I had to release it all. I think the nurse wondered what was going on and I didn't realise at the time, I was just taken aback with what she told me.

I went home, and the next day I ended my relationship with Matt. It was so hard to do and he was upset, but I knew it was right. I had feelings for someone else. I couldn't carry on the way things were; and I didn't have any other answers. He accepted my decision reluctantly and we parted. We had to keep in touch to sort out the division of the house and things but it was straight-forward. Matt was a decent guy and we agreed on the split of assets amicably.

We had had a lot of good times and experiences together but when one door closes as they say, another opens and that was the start of my relationship with David.

This was a massive turning point in my life. I had made the decision to start counselling (which remains part of my life) and so I was supported through the difficult break up with Matt.

Looking back, I realise that I had escaped my traumatic home life and dealt with the death of my father, both at a young age. I knew that my lowest point was the sleeping around with different guys, but it wasn't until my friendships started to break down that I realised that I needed to make some fundamental changes in my attitude and behaviour.

I began to realise that I had a lot of things to deal with, and I was at the beginning of my journey, with no idea as to how long I would be traveling for. At that time, I thought I would perhaps need a year or so of counselling, but that would be it.

Little did I know then, that the journey would still be going on today.

Insider Tip:

From what I know now, I have learnt that *generally* people won't make changes until things get extremely bad. The pain must be great enough to make them act. People fear coming out of their comfort zone and often think it's better to stay with what they know even though it's uncomfortable than face the fear of something new and the unknown.

Time to Reflect

Reflecting on my relationship with Matt is an interesting one. We were very much in love for a long time and we moved quite fast in terms of getting to know each other and then living together. He is a very kind person and helped me so much in terms of supporting me through my Dad's death. When we met he also helped me with my finances as I wasn't great at saving so I had a credit card bill I needed to pay and he just paid it off. It was the most generous thing anyone had ever done for me at that time in my life.

We both had our issues and I think that communication was something we struggled with. I thought I was good at it but in fact I wasn't very good at all. I was just telling him what the problem was, I wouldn't say how things made me feel most of the time. I would moan about his absence and his workaholic tendencies but never really understood it from his perspective.

If there was something wrong, we would often sit in silence and not talk about it. I would go over and over things in my head, conversations I wanted to have, things I wanted to say but never did. I got to the point where I felt it wouldn't have made a difference. There was a lot of frustration because I couldn't fix it. I felt I was the only one that had to do something, I thought it was my responsibility.

Knowing that we were both unhappy and often guessing at what was going on for Matt because he wouldn't say, really affected my mental health. I was constantly left worried, not knowing if I had done or said something to upset him. The more I asked the more stressed it made him, but I didn't know what was happening and my need to clear the air and talk was of utmost importance to me.

Living on eggshells was how I spent over 16 years and it seemed this was repeating itself. The parallels again are very like my home life with my family. Recently I looked at some research which explained that there isn't much difference with those that live with alcoholism and those that live with mental health in terms of the issues they faced.

It took a lot of courage but I know ending the relationship was the best thing I could have done, I did keep trying for a long time, probably far too long but at least I felt I did what I could.

Getting professional help at this stage was also a decision I wished I had come to a lot sooner but I wasn't ready for that, things hadn't got bad enough to push me to that point. It is a decision I will never ever regret and the best thing I did, the start of my transformation.

Chapter 15 – New Adventures

I'd been in my role at the insurance company for a year or so by the time I met David. I was living with a friend near to where I worked for a short period after moving out of the house with Matt, just whilst I got myself settled. David and I would talk on the phone for ages to each other and every call was exciting and great to hear his voice.

After my second trip to Dublin things changed a lot. David and I were chatting daily, each of us jetting back and forth to see each other. I love Dublin. It has a great atmosphere and of course I love the Irish accent so being immersed in that world was amazing. I got to know his family, stayed there when I went over, and he got to know my family and friends too.

After a while we had to decide about how to carry on. The excitement of flying over to Dublin was fun, but it wasn't something we could sustain. He decided to move to be with me (which I was eternally grateful for!) -he knew I didn't want to move and it was the only option.

He filled his car with his belongings and drove over via the ferry to me. It was one of the most exciting times of my life. We were head over heels in love with each other and it was full on from an early stage.

Initially Daisy let him stay at her house, which was great and we couldn't have managed without her. We all rented a place locally together to keep the costs down. At around that time In 2001 Daisy met Neil at her badminton club, he would come and stay over in the flat but things got a little heated and having all four of us in one place wasn't really working at times. Eventually we had to move because David's job was about an hour away and it was quite a commute for him so it worked out OK. Daisy and Neil moved into a place locally which all happened quite quickly after they first met but then it all happened fast for David and I too.

At the same time Mum started dating Simon. He used to work at The Moat House Hotel with all of us so we knew him, he used to be Daisy's boss when she was working in the kitchen. It was so odd that all three of us started new relationships around the same time.

David and I moved into a house near his job which saved him a lot of time in travel. He was a delivery driver for a large company and really loved it. He worked for them in Dublin so the transfer over was an easy one. He made friends but it took time, as he didn't know anyone apart from me, and my family. I don't think I appreciated how hard that was for him; he took all the risks and I'm not sure I showed him how much I appreciated that. Maybe it isn't until now that I can see just how much he did.

We did all the usual things people do in relationships; holidays, socialising with my friends and family. It was a little more difficult because we were quite a drive from my family who couldn't get to us easily. We went back to my home town quite a bit to see everyone. David got on well with

Daisy's partner, they were like twins. They looked similar and both enjoyed cars and doing the same things which was great as he needed male company. David was so funny and had us all in stitches on a regular basis, we all had a good sense of humour and it was nice to have a laugh as so much of our lives had been serious.

David and I lived away for about a year or so but the travelling took its toll and being away from our friends and family wasn't much fun and I was unhappy where we were living so we decided to move back to where my family were. I was still working for the insurance company so getting to work from either place wasn't an issue for me.

We started looking for places to buy because renting was such a waste of money, it took some time but we found place we liked. We started the process but the agents were mucking us around a bit, the flat was beautiful and we had our hearts set on it. We got the survey done and then the sellers pulled out. We were devastated and the time and money wasted was a little hard to swallow. At that time, I was so obsessive and would be onto the agents and chasing things up and making my own stress for myself.

Eventually I went to view another property and it was so much bigger than the last one. I loved it, bright rooms with lovely big windows. We put in an offer and got it, we were happy and within a few months we owned our first home together. There was a lot of work that needed doing, a new kitchen, bathroom, carpets and mainly decorative work but there was no rush.

At around the same time In 2002 Daisy and Neil bought a

place not far from Mum's flat. So we both moved around the same time, spooky that we met our partners and moved at the same sort of time.

Our relationship overall was fun, supportive and very loving. One of my favourite holidays with David was to Florida. We got a great deal and on arrival to pick up our car we were told we were entitled to an upgrade and ended up with a convertible. It made our day and we made use of having the roof down at every possible opportunity. David did the driving as he was more than happy to drive.

There was so much to see there, we went to all the usual stops. One of my favourites was visiting Animal Kingdom, inside was the set of Swiss Family Robinson which was one of the films we used to watch as kids repeatedly. I couldn't believe what I was seeing, the features were exactly like I remembered from the movie. I could have spent days there, so much to see and do.

We also visited Universal Studios, I love movies and David did too so we got to go on the sets of some of the movies that had been made. 'Backdraft' was one of them and it was amazing to see how all the stunts worked. I was absolutely fascinated, it was quite tiring as there were a lot of different areas and everything was so spread out.

We took lots of photos and were typical tourists on that front, we enjoyed lots of lovely food and they had a place called Pondarosa and it was a huge buffet place with lots of variety of food. You paid an entrance fee and could basically help yourself to whatever was inside.

It was Halloween time when went to Florida and so one evening we went to Universal Studios, it was the most amazing thing for Halloween I had experience and have experience to date. We walked through the turnstiles and for a moment I lost David, I looked around me and couldn't see him anywhere. There were hundreds of people and my heart started pumping and my throat and chest were getting tighter. I started to freak out as the time went on and I wasn't able to see him, I kept looking and eventually we found each other. I gave him the biggest hug and kept hold of him for the rest of the night.

We started to walk through the park and there were people on high stilts dressed up in extremely artistic outfits. We carried on walking and people were hiding in the bushes and would randomly jump out at us. The adrenalin was pumping; we decided to go into this haunted house.

Walking through the door we went into this big warehouse area which was split up into sections. We walked around the doored areas apprehensive of what was coming. I was hiding behind David all the way and jumping out of my skin when something unexpected happened. It was so odd; whilst I was scared I still wanted to continue, much like watching a horror movie behind a pillow but peeking over the top as you just want to know what is going to happen.

It was a great few hours and we took it all in, getting lots of photos and just enjoying being together. The Americans know how to go all out with events and attractions. It made me think how lame England can be in some of what they do.

We were in Florida for two lovely weeks and did as much as

we could in that time; 'Wet n Wild' waterpark was one of our favourites so we went there a few times. It was just nice to have time away together and enjoy each other's company.

David and I were so happy, he decided to change his job and become a driving instructor so I helped him with his course and used to go out in the car with him to support him. He had to go on a training course and on the course, he met one of his first friends, they got on like a house on fire. Unbelievably the guy lived nearby so after their initial meeting they kept in touch and would study together and go out and do practical sessions to make sure they both knew what they were doing.

It didn't take long before they both passed their exams and David started advertising his business to get some clients. I think the training centre helped them get clients but as with any business it was slow to start. At times, it was difficult because I was doing a lot in the house and I financially supported David whilst he wasn't working.

Some of the things that were important to me weren't a priority to David and anniversaries got forgotten, things around the flat we bought weren't getting done if I didn't do them. He was very used to his Mum and sisters doing everything for him at home. I started getting a little fed up of it and wanted him to help.

Relationships are about compromise, I was very controlling in the relationship but David would always stand up to me, he wasn't one for taking any crap which is just what I needed. Every relationship has its ups and downs and we didn't have that many for a long time.

David's business started to pick up and he had a regular intake of clients which was great and he was enjoying his work. I was proud of him and happy that he was doing something he felt was worthwhile and a career. He wanted more for himself than to be a delivery driver and I admired his motivation and ambition.

In 2002 Daisy had her first son George. It was an exciting time for the family, a grandchild for my Mum and I would be an Aunty. David and I had him to stay when he was only one or two days old so Daisy could get some sleep and recover. Neil was working so getting uninterrupted sleep as anyone with kids will know is a rarity. I remember it so clearly, I put him in the Moses basket next to the bed and I just kept waking up, making sure he was still breathing, it was ridiculous really but then I hadn't ever had a child and wasn't going to either so I had no idea what I was doing.

It was lovely that Daisy trusted me with George and I did enjoy the experience because he was so cute but it was lovely to be able to give him back to her. Daisy had always wanted kids for as far back as I can remember and she was in her element. Her dream had finally been fulfilled; she had a loving partner and her first child.

It took time for everything to settle and Daisy and Neil to find their feet but they did. Mum was the ever-doting grandmother and always there to help Daisy out when she needed it. She only lived up the road but not for long after George was born as she bought a place with Simon. It was a nice little bungalow, it was a little further out to where Daisy and I lived but was a nice place if not a bit small. It was fine for what they needed though.

George was so cute with his tiny little toes and fingers and I loved helping with changing him and looking after him whenever I had the chance.

After four years or so David and I started having other issues, I was running out of ideas of how to resolve them, I felt I was the one that had to come up with a solution but of course I wasn't, but my nature was to take on the responsibility myself.

We were due to go on holiday together and I decided that it was time to call it a day. Apart from the disagreements we were having the main reason was that he wanted children, and I didn't. Each of us probably thought the other would change their minds but neither of us did. It was so sad because he was an amazing person. I told him I wanted to split up and he got angry and chucked the money at me for the holiday, I knew he was upset and I didn't know what to say. I felt apprehensive and on edge before I told him, wondering when was the best time and the answer to that is never.

It took me a long time to get to this point because I did my very best to be the person I thought he wanted in the relationship, but I wasn't being me. There wasn't any point lying to myself or him anymore, I wanted different things from the relationship and it wasn't fair to expect him to be someone he wasn't and he wasn't the type of person to compromise himself anyway, which is a good thing to a point.

When things were getting difficult, I found it increasingly hard to manage the relationship. I realise now that I wasn't as good at expressing my feelings as I thought. I found it difficult to accept difference; I see things in black and white and it was extremely hard to deal with people that behaved in a way I disliked.

This is much like my parents. To them I was 'different' and they found me difficult to deal with. It was the counselling I was having that taught me that I could never change anyone - that if things were not right, then the person who had to change was me.

I have always needed to have the answers. I realised I needed to be better at discussing things to try and find solutions. Most importantly, I needed to learn that those solutions never come straight away. I can be impatient.

During the troubles in my relationship with David I started chatting to a man at work. We got on well - he was older than me but we connected on a psychological level and enjoyed discussing self-help.

Thus, I made an awful mistake, one I regret to this day. I started a relationship with a man at work called Mark *before* I ended things with David. Once we had split up I did tell him that I had cheated on him (probably to relieve my own guilt) because I knew he was finding the split difficult and in my mind this would make it easier for him. I knew he would never want to talk to me again as he was stubborn about certain things and this was certainly one of them.

David and I had to go through splitting the property and so on which was upsetting and difficult. He decided to move back to Dublin as there was nothing keeping him in Bournemouth any longer. Because I was fascinated with my new man I didn't allow myself to grieve properly or give myself the time I needed to deal with the end of this relationship.

Of course, I could have dealt with things differently. I felt pressured by Mark because he wanted me to himself and I felt he was threatened and jealous of David. It was my choice to do what I did and it gave me what I needed at the time, no matter how selfish I was being it made me feel good until the guilt kicked in. So, David and I ended and we both started our new lives. It's sad to think that David is not seeing George grow up as George does remember him, but it wasn't to be.

Chapter 16 – A New Relationship

It was 2005 when I met Mark, I blamed myself for what had happened with David. I knew he hated me for the betrayal (and probably still does). The fact I have tried and failed to communicate with him since bears this out. I tried to send him messages and to talk but he never responds.

As time went on it got easier, and the guilt subsided a bit. I had my new relationship, although this wasn't ideal either. Mark was married with two children and so the guilt crept up again. After several months, he eventually left his wife. It was all handled delicately because of the children but he moved out to his mother's house and we continued our relationship at a distance – it was a two-hour drive to see each other.

I was still working in the purchasing/administrative role but I wanted something more challenging so I volunteered for a Trainer position. There was a lot of requirement in the businesses across the UK for Microsoft Word, Excel and Outlook training and I loved computers so it made sense.

It was an exciting time for me because it gave me something to get my teeth into but it would mean a lot of travel. The offices in the group were spread all over the place with the head office in Kent and the IT head office in Essex. We also had another IT department in London. I remember spending so much time in my car, travelling up and down the country and on the phone to my friends and family to chat about my day or love life issues. They were all very supportive and it was nice to have them on the end of the phone.

To say I didn't have some funny incidents would be an understatement, because my anxiety was still very much in full swing at that time I used to get exceptionally nervous when going to new places because I didn't know what to expect. Often, I would leave home or leave the office I was working in to travel somewhere and then need the toilet, and isn't it typical when you need to go and there is no toilet to be found. I often had to stop on the motorway to relieve myself, it was so embarrassing and I recall driving down the road eyeing up the hard shoulder looking for bushes and trees and wondering where I could stop where I wouldn't be seen.

It became a bit of a joke to my family and friends, always needing to go to the toilet. Sometimes I would pass a service station and think I'll be OK I don't need it yet and then BAM, a traffic jam. Oh, my goodness did I learn fast that if I feel any inclination then I need to pull over. I had no idea some of it was related to my anxiety but it totally makes sense now.

Over the years of working at the insurance company it grew very quickly and we inherited IT staff from the companies we bought so that is why the logistics were as they were.

The travelling was an enjoyable part of my life if not a little stressful at time., Towards the end of that role we merged with another IT group of trainers and the remit of my role changed to training in insurance applications which wasn't something I was interested in so I was lucky enough to be able to change my role back to doing IT Procurement.

Where we could we spent our time commuting back and forth, Mark would visit me and I would visit him once he had found his own place. It was exciting finishing work on a Friday and leaving to go up and see him or know he was coming to see me. As we worked in the same company and he was the boss we managed to organise the logistics of work with our private life so it made it slightly easier.

When I was staying at his we would drive into the office together, I won't lie it felt good. I was dating the boss and I was proud of it, I suppose it made me feel like I had done well for myself.

Work colleagues eventually found out we were dating after I accidentally let it slip at a work Christmas party to one of Mark's staff's wife. I didn't want to keep it a secret and I should've been more careful because he was still married and it could have made things very difficult. Over the period of our relationship it did get difficult, staff at work wouldn't speak to me about things for fear I would tell him or they would tell me something knowing I would pass it on or hope I would for their benefit.

When we weren't at work we both enjoyed doing similar things, he was in a band and at that time I wasn't really doing much singing but it would have been fun to sing in his band. I remember him practising at his house and I went to a couple of public gigs he did, he was very good. He enjoyed the release after a stressful day at work but often it was difficult to get everyone together for practice.

At the weekends, we would go for walks down the beach if he came to me, catch up with my friends or go out for dinner. We did take some nice breaks away as well which was a real treat. We went to Paris and Amsterdam which was great fun.

Mark took me on my first ever skiing trip which was amazing and scary at the same time, I had some lessons at the local dry ski resort but it wasn't a lot. Mark booked us into a lovely place in Chamonix and we didn't arrive until late and there was no one there to let us in, eventually we managed to get hold of someone and got ourselves settled and headed to bed.

The next day we got out on the slopes, Mark was extremely competitive and bearing in mind I hadn't skied before I wasn't exactly up for a slalom. The weather wasn't great it was snowing heavily and neither of us had googles on, we couldn't see our hand in front of our face at one stage so we had to invest in some googles so we could see where we were going.

The ski boots were really hurting my shins and I was struggling to walk even first thing in the morning. I had obviously done some damage but Mark was keen to get skiing so we ventured back onto the slopes for more. I got very frustrated and angry, probably more at myself than him as I really wasn't fit to be on the slopes. I was in total agony and it got so bad we had to go to the shops to see if there was something they could give me. I had these gel type cushions to put on my shins which helped but it was still painful. I think it was probably shin splints but at the time I just knew it hurt like hell.

This first trip could have been amazing but unfortunately, I really felt my confidence go. Mark was fine on the snow and used to it but I didn't know how to handle being on ice and navigating tricky situations. I'm no risk taker so letting go wasn't easy for me to do. My legs were certainly happy to have a rest when it came to the end of the holiday, the scenes were beautiful and I managed to get lots of pictures. I did enjoy stopping off each day for lovely croissants and hot wine, a real treat.

After our holiday, It wasn't always easy physically being in the same place but we were on the phone to each other all the time and often for hours at a time.

The conversation did tend to fluctuate from work to personal and it was hard to keep the two separate. We did try and when we caught ourselves getting caught up with issues at work Mark would remind us that we needed to change the subject and that some things he obviously couldn't talk about to me.

Where he lived was beautiful, it was an old cottage that he bought and it had a massive garden. The house had low ceilings and lovely oak beams and the lounge had an Inglenook fireplace. It wasn't at all like where I lived but it was a nice contrast, it was so cosy in the winter with the fire blazing.

We would walk up the road to the local pub and enjoy a Sunday lunch or dinner of an evening on the nights I stayed at his house, on a weekend we would go to the local shop which was posh. They sold homemade chutneys, cheese and offered vegetables, wine and all sorts. We use to buy this amazing duck pate and would serve it on fresh crunchy baguette with some chutney on the top and it was just divine.

Mark was an amazing cook and he use to whip up some delicious creations for me, I felt a bit useless to be honest but he did look after me. We made a real thing of going to the supermarket and picking up the ingredients for a meal and whilst I couldn't afford all the high-quality items Mark wanted I made the best contribution I could. We just agreed that I would give what I would usually pay and he made up the rest, it seemed to work for us.

We would get back to the house and he would get cracking on the dinner and I would help with the cocktails which were an amazing accompaniment to the meal. We'd sit in front of the blazing fire watching TV and just relax, it was total bliss.

Dating someone you work with has its challenges, especially as throughout the time we were together he was my boss. I loved his intellect as he was clever when it came to IT and he knew a lot about psychology and people. We had endless talks about the topic as at the time I was still in therapy and reading self-development books.

His charm was what won me over most of the time, he knew how to say the right things at the right time. I found dating the boss exhilarating, it was interesting to see another side of my company and the things he had to deal with. I'd get to go to things I probably wouldn't have done if I wasn't dating him.

In 2005, Daisy had another baby called Thomas. They had moved to a new house not far from my flat. It was lovely to have another baby arriving in the family. Things weren't as easy for Daisy and Neil to get out and about and everyone's lives changed a little bit more in terms of interests and doing the same things. A few years after Thomas was born it became apparent that something wasn't quite right and eventually he was diagnosed with autism.

The only thing I really noticed was that he wasn't particularly cuddly and wouldn't really interact with us and I remember feeling I didn't have much of a relationship with him as he really would only go to Daisy. We didn't know it then but this was going to be the start of a very difficult time for Daisy and her family.

Chapter 17 – Cracks Started Appearing

Unfortunately, things didn't always run smoothly with Mark, I used to go out with friends at the weekend when I was at home and I believe Mark felt jealous and concerned that I was going to go off with someone else. It put a lot of pressure on the relationship, cracks started to seep in and things got a little intense. I genuinely wasn't interested in anyone else and so I didn't feel his fear wasn't based on anything I did.

One occasion I was out with a friend in town and got a text message on my phone saying I looked "mighty fine tonight", I thought the person must know who I was as they used my name. I texted back trying to find out who it was but they wouldn't reveal themselves. I carried on my evening but I was mentally torturing myself about who it might be, I was getting more anxious and couldn't really enjoy my evening.

My friend told me to stop responding to the text messages but I was hooked on the intrigue and the person made me feel that they were in Bournemouth and following me and would meet me in the next bar, which never happened. I decided to stop texting as I was getting more and more wound up and it was ruining my night out.

I found out whose phone it was and there was a connection to Mark, I've never had the facts from Mark which left me feeling very confused and left wondering what really went on.

This incident left me extremely scared and I felt totally bewildered. I felt like I was going mad, I questioned myself, I doubted myself, I reassured myself that Mark wasn't involved, I went around and around in circles. I didn't know what to believe and his stories always sounded so plausible.

To me he had all the power and at times I felt like the confused child in the relationship, which is probably what I was at times. I felt a little brain washed and at the time I felt like Mark was being manipulative and controlling. It can happen to even the strongest people and I would consider myself a strong person.

Eventually we moved on from the incident but we were split up for a while and then got back together. This wasn't the only incident, on the contrary there are too many to mention and thankfully now I am in a much better place and don't believe I would ever let that sort of thing happen to me. Thankfully I've got more self-esteem and respect for myself to allow others to mistreat me.

Sadly, there were other events which just caused me to doubt the quality of the relationship and if we should be together. The phone calls that lasted hours with Mark trying to convince me of his view, he once turned up unannounced because I didn't want to speak to him and he wouldn't respect my decision. He would keep calling and calling until I had to disconnect my phone. I really did fear him at times and the parallels of the relationship with him and my father were uncanny. I don't know what was going on for him and there are two sides to every story, he acted that way for a reason.

We went to a wedding reception of his friends at a low point of our relationship and he wasn't being very nice to me which I do understand because he was probably very frustrated that he was putting in a lot of effort and I wasn't as committed as him. I just found him too controlling and I was very mixed up and didn't know what I wanted. We arrived at the wedding reception and he went off and chatted to his friend and I was just left alone. I couldn't find him anywhere and I had no clue what to do.

We were staying at the hotel and so I went back to the room to see if he was there but he wasn't. Eventually I ended up in tears in the ladies' toilets, I was overwhelmed with emotion. Not just about that situation but a whole host of past issues. I eventually found him and heard him talking on the phone in our bedroom so I walked in and asked him where he'd been, he was evasive and wouldn't say too much. I suspected there was someone else but I had no proof, my mind was often going off by itself coming up with scenarios and causing me more worry than I needed.

The mental torture in the relationship was the worst part, in part this was my own doing, over-analysing and putting my own ideas on what was going on. I don't think I was mentally reacting and behaving as an adult a lot of the time. I responded in a more childlike way and had a sense of naivety around me. I wanted to believe what he said, I had hope that things would be OK but I was just kidding myself.

We would swing from getting on and being nice to each other to despising each other. It rarely happened at the same time, I would try and seek his approval, love and forgiveness and then he would do the same to me. The relationship was toxic.

One of the final points of the relationship was went we went for a skiing trip with my friends. The week was strained and we had disagreements and I was making hurtful comments and it just wasn't the loving relationship I would have liked. He was often logging into work to look at emails and deal with any issues that might have arisen in his absence. It wasn't until our return from the holiday that I discovered he'd been chatting to another woman.

I was at crisis point in this relationship; it was 2007 by the time I finally ended things and whilst it wasn't an amicable split there were still times when we would be in touch but it got less and less as time went on.

Just before we split up I decided to move back into the purchasing department because all the travel was taking its toll and I wanted to be based out of Bournemouth again. It was a relief not to have to rearrange my life around work and jet off at a moment's notice. The novelty of staying in hotels and living out of a packed bag had passed me by.

Time to Reflect

This relationship ended up being one of the most toxic relationships of my life. We were both controlling people. I was still vulnerable from the breakdown of my previous relationship, and he was in a position of power at work. At times, I felt this was used in our relationship. If he pushed I pulled, if he didn't show interest in me I would do things to get attention, if I didn't give him the attention he needed he would look elsewhere or act out, he was jealous and I felt manipulated by him. We certainly didn't bring out the best in each other that's for sure.

I learnt a lot about myself in the time we were together, which was two years on and off. I do feel sorry for all the friends who had to listen to our relationship woes because there were many!

We were addicted to each other, we knew it wasn't healthy but couldn't stop, you may see the parallels here. He was my addiction; it was like a drug, and even though I knew it wasn't good for me I kept going back for more. He gave me the affection that I craved which was absent from my childhood, he had the same authority figure status as my father, the same high expectations. He would lecture me (that's what it felt like) just like my Dad did in the kitchen and it would go on for hours just like Dad would.

This was one of the lowest points in my life. No other situation before or since has made me feel the way I did in those two years. The reason I felt like this about the relationship was because it was mentally exhausting. It caused my anxiety to rocket through the roof and I felt like I was a prisoner in my own relationship.

Continually questioning myself and not being able to decide for fear of the consequences. Having to think about everything I said and how I worded it because it would be analysed to death and taken out of context. When I say, I felt I was going mad that is probably not far off the truth, I know Daisy was extremely worried about me. I was reading a lot of self-help books to understand what was going wrong, what I was doing wrong. It got obsessive and I think that is what I do when I'm struggling to cope.

Insider Tip

Those affected by someone's drinking are likely to experience relationship issues. They tend to recreate the dysfunctional patterns of relating in the present which mirrors unresolved issues from the past. This was true for me I was transferring issues from my Dad with Mark.

At a different time and place it probably would have been a very different relationship and whilst it was a disaster we did manage to clear the air after some years. We both apologised for our behaviour and I feel some peace about it all now.

To be honest, I just didn't know what to do and where to turn. I doubted myself - the more I read about human behaviour the more I thought I was 'broken' and couldn't be 'fixed'.

I found myself asking all my friends and family for their opinion as I couldn't decide about anything. I knew my last relationship had affected me negatively but it taught me a lot as well; and I believe in reflecting on things that happen to explore what we need to learn.

Self Help Tip:

Reflection: Not often given the time of day but so very important. Taking the time to reflect on your day, a situation, an experience can be extremely insightful. You can do this in so many ways, through pictures, recording yourself, writing in a diary are just a few.

It's important to remember this is my view and experience and I can't speak for Mark and know things from his side. It wasn't all bad and I think we were both ashamed of our behaviour in the relationship at times.

Self-help books ruled my life for quite some time. I thought they held all the answers and would read them cover to cover, highlighting important parts so I wouldn't forget what I needed to know. Ironically now I realise that whatever is important to us we will remember, the rest we forget and let go.

My thinking totally consumed me. I became much more analytical and deep thinking. Imagine reading a first aid book and finding that you match all the symptoms. One of my many therapists suggested I stop reading them - probably the best thing I did.

Chapter 18 – Friendships

Whilst I've talked about childhood friends and my friends at college over the years I've had several friendships that have lasted but a lot that haven't. This was an area of my life that was extremely difficult for me and each friendship had its own issues and of course learning.

Today I'm blessed to have a myriad of very good friends. My best friend Sammy has been there for me throughout my life since college and I love her dearly. She is eccentric, fun, genuine and will bring you back down to earth in an instant. She tells it like it is and doesn't try to be someone she isn't. It's probably the easiest and longest friendship I've had, she doesn't take life too seriously which is the opposite to me and she's very empathic to others, always seeing life from their viewpoint. I'm lucky to have her and after 25 years of friendship I'm so grateful that she gave me a chance instead of listening to other's opinion of me.

Hayley and I got together when I was single and so was she at the time and we supported each other through the tough times, she was on her own with two very young children. We started a catering business together for a short while but it was a lot harder than we thought and we decided to knock it on the head, it was fun but not meant to be. She's also my hairdresser and so a clever lady, she's an amazing person and always helping others, sometimes to her own detriment but she's grown so much over the years and I'd like to think my positive influence has helped her.

Laura is an amazing woman that I met when I started my therapy business and we met at a network event, she is a community musician as well as wearing a few different hats. Probably one of the most talented women I know, she has invested so much of her time and energy into helping me and I never really feel I give it back to her in equal helpings. She's honest which I love, no nonsense but incredibly intelligent. What she doesn't know about music isn't worth knowing and don't get her started on Gabriel Byrne. She's easy to be around, full of useful insights, wise, did I mention amazing? She is the lady that is helping me edit this book and write a song about my Dad. She's got a great business head and we both share a love of psychology.

Lucy is my friend from when I worked on the tourism project. Whilst we haven't been friends for that many years I value our friendship greatly. She is a lot younger than me but we really get on, I think we have a similar sense of humour and enjoy the same things. She doesn't live in the same town as me but we catch up when we can, she is very understanding and kind and I love that about her. She is always there if I need a chat and is never judgmental about anything.

Emmy is my friend from college and whilst we had many years when we didn't speak because I was immature and a complete bitch and possibly as her husband told me recently a 'psycho' we have got back in touch over the past years which has been amazing and I'm very grateful that she has forgiven me. Emmy is the sweetest person you'll meet, very giggly and fun. At times I can confess I feel quite inadequate because she never complains about anything really. Most of my friends will have a moan about relationships, work or someone cutting them up but Emmy never does. Now we have been back in touch we have both developed a love of football so whenever I can get her and her husband and son a ticket I do. It's great that we have grown closer over the years and I can only put that down to her patience and forgiveness and my hard work on building a better me.

My friend Michelle is someone I've known since I was 3, we went to the same nursery, junior and senior school and we were as thick as thieves at school but as life went on we lost touch and over the years we have just got back in touch and then fallen out of contact again. Michelle is so funny and we have a great laugh together, we have always had a good time together and she's so kind and thoughtful towards others and has a very close family who I've known for years. Thankfully we are still in touch now and it amazes me after so many years that we have managed to keep that friendship going. We both support the same football team and so usually natter about that as well as what's going on in our lives. Michelle has 2 kids as do most of my friends, I think I'm the only one that doesn't have any children. I can't imagine we'll ever not speak, so I'm looking forward to seeing how well we age over the years!

Melanie is my friend from school but who I went out with while working at the hotel in the evenings. I used to live with her and her Mum for a while too. We have been friends for about 25 years on and off. My friendship with Melanie has been turbulent over the years, mainly due to my instability and at times being a complete head case. When I was younger I idolised her because she is very glamourous, had a car and lived a very attractive life. She was ALWAYS there to listen to me moan on about my boyfriends and get myself in a state. We used to enjoy going out shopping on a Saturday and then venture out in the evenings for drinks and some dancing. There are far too many stories to tell!

I met Louise through a friend of Melanie's that I got to know and we got on well as she was a fun and carefree character. She lives near London and we only see each other a few times a year but it's nice. We had our ups and downs and times where we didn't speak but I contacted her a few years ago because I wanted to resolve the issues we once faced, I'm so pleased that she agreed to keep in touch because she could have just ignored me. Whilst we are quite different we also have some similarities, she is very honest like me so we often laugh about the faux pas we have made. We are also both very kind and like to do things for other people, she loves to travel and is super independent like me. Even though they'll be months where we don't speak it doesn't matter, we'll pick up the phone and catch up and have a good natter.

When I went out with Liam I got to know his step-sister Reece quite well, we had similar interests in terms of business and self-development although she became a lot more interested in spiritualism than me but we got on well. We both supported each other through the start-up of our businesses, she now has a very successful salon and has started up another company offering amazing massage products and training to beauty salons and I feel extremely proud of her. We lost touch for a period of time because we fell out over something stupid to do with my business, although it's never just about that is it. I think I found her brutal honesty hard at

137

times which was interesting because I'm the same! Thankfully we have regained our friendship and are still supporting each other in our businesses today.

I met Amy at a festival that I went to, we went to work there to help out a lady that offered beauty and hair treatments to people in the festival. It was a bit of a disaster but I got to meet Amy and she was really fun, she had a sensitive side and we got on well. We chatted about her boyfriend at the time as she was having some problems so I put my counsellor hat on to offer some advice. We didn't really keep in touch much after that but in the recent year or two we have become closer friends. She is only 26 but has a wise head on her shoulders. I like her honesty and what you see is what you get. We have a laugh together which is important and I admire her morals and values. She treats people well and is very respectful towards others which I like.

Some of my friends I've had for years and others I've developed more recently in my life. A few of them have been business colleagues initially and then we have developed a friendship which I'm so thankful for. They've been so generous with the time and helped me in my business and where possible I help them. I've met friends through the choir and singing past and present, swimming and work.

If I reflect on my friendships in my adult life I can probably sum up a lot of the challenges I've faced, some I've overcome and some I haven't. Most of the time the issues I have had with my friends is generally centred around my expectations of them, not doing what I think they should or what they say they will and behaving in a way I don't think is right.

Obviously, I have no right to expect this of others, but none of us are perfect right? If I turn this around I have high expectations and standards of myself so I transfer that onto others and I probably don't always behave in a way my friends like. I know my honest and brutal opinions have also caused issues over the years, I tell people the truth but it isn't always what they want to hear. I never used to have any tact but over the years I have managed to get better, not perfect but that is who I am and I must accept the consequences of my behaviour.

My communication at times has probably not been as specific as it could've been and then arrangements have got misinterpreted. I end up feeling angry and frustrated and disappointed. At times I've also taken on far too much responsibility and then when things don't go to plan I find it difficult to adjust to it. Learning to be more patient, understanding and apply some compassionate is a work in progress.

Friends and family are everything and without them, life can be lonely and boring. We can't always get on all the time, but I believe if communication is open and honest the relationship will be so much better and I tend to feel more relaxed. I'd rather know if someone wasn't happy and for us to understand it from each other's perspective so it doesn't happen again. If it does there is more empathy there but I know a lot of people don't like confrontation.

Personally I don't like confrontation but I do it because my need to resolve issues is greater than my fear of facing the awkwardness.

Chapter 19 – Wake Up

Whilst my relationship was ending Daisy and Neil's was continuing to thrive as they decide to get married. I was a bridesmaid and whilst Daisy was getting ready at my flat Neil, Mum, Simon and I were at the wedding reception venue getting the place ready for after the ceremony. It looked nice but it was quite stressful, time was running out and we had left it quite late to get back to get ready.

Getting myself into my bridesmaid outfit was a rush, thankfully Daisy had our brother Joe there to keep her company. Daisy's friend was the photographer so got some nice photos of us all in my lounge and then within about 30 minutes we had to be out of the flat and making our way to the Town Hall.

There were some heated moments with Mum and I lost my temper, we were arguing about the lack of time and everyone was just under pressure. Daisy felt like she was on her own and no one to share the fun with in terms of getting ready. We should have asked other people to help but hindsight is a wonderful thing.

Mum's friend took Daisy in the car with Joe and arrived at the Town Hall with everyone waiting for their arrival. I had some pictures taken outside the front and some nice ones of Mum and Simon too.

The ceremony was nice and very emotional, my big sister was finally getting married.

We all made our way to the sports club for the evening, the best part of a wedding. It was fun and George and Thomas enjoyed a bit of dancing with their friends, as well as chasing each other around the room. The evening was fun and the music was good. It all seemed to go so fast.

It soon came to the time when I had to make my speech. I thought I would embarrass myself by sharing a story about how Daisy decided to tie me to a tree outside our house in Capstone Road when I was young because I annoyed her. She stuffed peanuts up my nose and something in my mouth so I couldn't breathe very well and just left me there. The room filled with laughter. As the evening came to an end, we all said our goodbyes to family and friends and thanked them for coming.

It was a long day and I was so glad to get to bed and get some much-needed sleep.

In the aftermath of the relationship with Mark, it wasn't long before I started seeing another guy at work called Sam. I was still having therapy on and off and reading self-help books to try and find answers, to help me understand what went wrong in my relationships and how I could fix myself.

My need to change and understand myself and others was a direct result of wanting to be accepted by my mother and father. I wanted to be the person they wanted me to be, the one that they would be proud of and love but it doesn't work like that. This was their issue, their total lack of ability to accept me for who I was and love me unconditionally.

Throughout my life, I've needed the support of therapy, of something that was going to help me get through the bad times, and counselling is where I found my solace. It was another addiction. I hated things not being fixed – if something is broken I want to fix it, a characteristic I developed growing up. It gave me the sense of control which I never had at home.

We all develop characteristics, behaviours, values and beliefs based on our environment and experiences, and the people in our life. Whatever your background, these will have a direct impact - some good and some not so healthy. It's up to us to decide to do something about it, when we realise there is an issue. Some people just want to cope with a situation and others want to change it, the latter is a lot rarer.

Children of alcoholics rarely face their feelings; and many never realise how they have developed and adapted through living in such an environment. I had no idea about my mannerisms and behaviour until many years later. I had never heard of the term 'Adult Child of an Alcoholic' back then.

For many years, I just knew things weren't right for me, either in the relationships I was in or the friendships I had. I had problems with people in all areas of my life, and that's why I wanted to get help - to improve both myself and my situation.

The relationship with Sam lasted a couple of years from 2007 to 2009. He headed up the purchasing department so yet again I was working for my boyfriend. Initially we had a lot of fun, he was very laid back but had a passion and energy about him that I loved. I often find that people aren't as outwardly excited, passionate and energetic as me and it's nice to find someone that is.

We had some great times, we went skiing together which was a little easier after having done it once before. Sam had a good sense of humour if not a little immature at times which over a period did grate on me. When we were away he struggled to get off the ski lift and decided that pushing against me was a good idea. Basically, his snowboard ended up in my ribs and I later found out when I got back that I he'd broken them. It was very painful and I had to try and ski back down to a lift, thankfully it was towards the end of the holiday so I could get seen relatively quickly at home, not that there is anything they could do about it.

Sam loved being active like me, he played golf with the guys at work, loved shopping which was unusual for a bloke and loved his VW's. He bought an old VW Beetle when we were together and spent a fortune doing it up, it was a lovely baby blue and cream colour. His friend helped him and it was a major project as the car wasn't in great shape. It did look nice when it was done and he couldn't wait to get to some of the VW shows.

Unfortunately for me they all involved camping and it wasn't one of my favourite past times. I can just about manage caravans but every time I go camping it's either chucking it down and awful weather or boiling hot. I hate that I can't easily wash and so after doing a few I resisted doing any more.

143

We did quite a few of the festivals and one of the best ones was Santa Pod. It was great fun and in the evening, they had huge tents for music and dancing, we went with some friends so it was a great laugh.

In the time we were together, Sam became good friends with a girl at work, I knew her too and would go out with her occasionally. We would spend time outside of work going out for drinks and a few of us from the office went to London for the weekend for a bit of ice skating around Christmas time, had some drinks and dinner. It was a great group of people and generally we all got on.

One weekend Sam, my friend Louise and Jo from London and a few people from work and my friend Melanie all went to Butlins for a weekend. It was an 80's event so we all dressed up in our 80's outfits. It was a great laugh, we had a couple of apartments, the boys in one and the girls in the other. They were selling vodka slush puppies which were delicious. Lots of fun was had and lots of sore heads the next day.

Generally it was quite an active relationship, we were always doing something and going somewhere. Working so closely together was difficult. I could keep things separate at work but he found it hard. He often wanted to go into another room and talk about things that we were going through but I didn't want to because it was work and I didn't want people knowing anything about our private life. The atmosphere wasn't nice and I felt really on edge.

Sam was having issues with Mark who was his boss and as you can probably guess it was a very difficult situation. Eventually he went up to London and had a chat with Mark and they decided that he would leave the company.

After that there were a few roles that he worked at. One of them was in Milton Keynes, it was so far away and he was very annoyed that I didn't want to move there with him but my life and family were in Bournemouth and I wasn't prepared to up sticks and leave. I did go up to his house there and stay with him, it was nice enough. He shared it with a few others and in the summer he had some barbeques which were nice. They also had a proper snow dome with real snow so we use to go there at the weekends which was good and allowed me to get some practice in.

The stresses and strains of my relationship with Mark and the difficulties that brought to work and the interference with my relationship with Sam was tough on us all. None of us behaved particularly maturely if I'm honest but it was what it was. I became a little stressed with his friendship with the girl at work and went through his emails and found things about me that weren't very nice.

On reflection I was probably looking to sabotage the relationship because I wasn't happy with him. Even when he eventually found a job back in Bournemouth and moved into my place it wasn't right. He only stayed in my flat for a week or two, it was a lot of hassle with him moving everything, sorting out renting a garage for all his things and adjusting to being back in Bournemouth. I felt so bad after deciding that I didn't want to be with him that I moved out of my own flat to my sisters until he found somewhere to go.

It's funny because I realise how I was still putting others before me, I'm not sure any of my other friends would have done that. I know I wouldn't do that now, I just felt pressured into doing things I didn't want to and I wasn't being honest with Sam or myself.

During all this, I was still in therapy and soon came to realise that I was repeating old patterns. We seem to attract the same type of people, and at that time I was always looking for people I could 'fix', not that they wanted that.

None of this was my partner's fault; it was just how I went into relationships. I grew up thinking I wasn't 'OK' (there is a book called 'I'm OK you're OK", and what I mean by that is that I wasn't accepting myself) so I thought I had to become something else to be 'OK' and be accepted by the other person. This is clearly not the best way to go about things but I didn't know any different. I'd been conditioned into believing that I needed to change. My Dad never stopped asking me.

My lost identity wasn't something I was consciously aware of at the time; I was forever changing who I was, depending on which relationship I was in. I found it exhausting. Trying to be and act in a way I thought would suit the other person is fruitless. After a while it would become hard to keep doing that, not that I was aware of that at the time. Then I would get to a point where I started to feel resentful, because I wasn't being true to myself. I wasn't being me.

Often, I would get to the point where I felt I was giving a lot to the relationship but not getting much back - not the things I needed. I picked relationships with people that ultimately could not fulfil my needs; and we were never compatible. It's of course important to have different interests, and be independent, but underneath you need to be able to be yourself and be accepted as that person.

My partners probably accepted me but because I was *pretending* to be what they wanted I was lying to myself. Eventually the day always came when I realised they were not what I needed or wanted.

Insider Tip:

Those affected by someone's drinking become good at being people pleasers and putting others needs ahead of their own because living with a heavy drinker that is what you get used to.

Looking back at all my relationships with men the pattern is clear to me. I would use sex as a way of getting attention; and then enjoyed getting to know new people; but these always became relationships which were destructive to all concerned. My lack of self-worth and self-esteem always took its toll - I allowed men to treat me poorly, and of course I wasn't treating myself well either.

I feel like my body has been through so much and I didn't look after it in my twenties. I had no respect for myself and put myself into dangerous and unhealthy situations because of it. It saddens me now to think that is how I treated myself, but I understand the reasons for it. Thankfully I now have a different perspective on myself and life; and that is all down to the positive changes I decided to take.

Life with the rest of the family was always up and down, various things going on with Mum and Daisy. One thing I can say is that when the chips are down we are always there for each other, we are a small but close family even though we've had our differences.

It wasn't all bad, I managed to get a promotion in 2008 to Purchasing Manager and I had two staff to help me run the department, it was a great achievement for me and recognition for all my hard work.

Beautiful views from the mountain in Andorra

Bit of skiing

My attempt at making a snow angel

Time to Reflect

There is a lot of learning from every relationship, situation and experience. Sometimes it's not until years later that we learn lessons and have breakthrough moments. Often the people and situations we find the hardest are the lessons we need to learn the most.

The experiences I had were tough at the time and I hated being in them, because they caused me to feel uncomfortable and I didn't know how to 'sit' with those uncomfortable feelings. Now when things don't go to plan or as I'd like I'm better able to cope and know that it will pass and there'll be something to learn in there if I choose to see it. Mindfulness and Al-Anon has played a key part in that for me.

My relationships taught me a huge amount about myself and others, sometimes not until years later. I have also reflected on situations which have made me cringe and feel a little embarrassed, guilty or ashamed of my behaviour. As the years went on and my self-awareness increased I was more able to accept that it wasn't all my fault and I dealt with it in a calmer way as I got older.

Not being able to properly express myself and my feelings in my relationships was something that really shocked me when I finally realised I wasn't very good at it. Showing that vulnerable side of me wasn't something I felt comfortable with, even if it was with someone I had been with years.

Often I would go through life doing things I didn't want to do, for others and compromising myself. I rarely stopped to think, do I want to do 'x' and will that give me time for myself and am I considering 'Y'. I would just put others first and do whatever they needed because this gave me something, it gave me fulfilment. Eventually I learnt to consider myself, think things through before committing and allowing myself time.

Thinking about it, jealousy was very present in my relationships. Initially I felt jealous of Neil's relationship with Daisy and how that would affect my time with my sister, then when Daisy had children I felt jealous of the time she had to spend with them. I also felt jealousy towards other women with my partners, this just connects to my total lack of self-esteem and self-worth because I don't feel it so much now.

Chapter 20 - NLP

After a few years in therapy, in 2009 I discovered an assertiveness course that was running locally. I'm a confident person now but in certain situations then I was finding myself not assertive but aggressive. I had so much anger about what had happened to me as a child and that carried on through my life. In fact, I wasn't being assertive at all, I was aggressive to people and that's why they were responding in the way they were.

The course was enjoyable and it was a good experience, it was here I first heard about Neuro Linguistic Programming (NLP). I was intrigued and so I thought I'd find out more. I contacted the local Adult Learning Centre and booked myself onto an eight-week course. I love to learn, so it seemed a perfect next step.

Strangely enough I don't recall many of the details of the course; but the trainer was exceptionally clever and engaging. I decided to find out more about NLP and the trainer suggested I attend his practitioner training. This was run over nine non-consecutive weekends but it was a commitment I thought was worth it.

I shared what I was learning with friends but people that aren't into self-help didn't get the fascination. For me however the course was another one of the changing points in my life. I went for answers; I wanted to change and be a better person and I'd pinned my hopes on everything I was trying. Whether it was the books, the counselling sessions, courses, whatever - I was waiting for a 'Eureka' moment where everything would be solved and clear. It doesn't quite work like that.

When I first started reading self-help books I recall the phrase 'there is no quick fix' - essentially change takes time. Of course, I thought I was different and that I would sort myself out quickly, I had to, I was doing everything I needed to, wasn't I?

On the NLP course, there were people from all walks of life all attending for different reasons. On the first day, we were given a piece of paper with a list of instructions. One of the instructions was 'Find someone in the room that has been arrested'. I was a bit shocked, but it was an interesting exercise and a good way of getting to know a bit more about people.

The classes included discussions and demonstrations on different psychotherapeutic techniques. NLP is about influencing how our brain behaves through language and other methods of communication. It is about us 'recoding' the way our brain responds to things to develop new and improved behaviours.

We learnt quite a few techniques. One of my favourites was the 'Meta Model'. This is about the language we use; and how to challenge statements that people habitually make, often unconsciously. By doing this they have to think about what they've said and think about it differently. They can then hopefully realise that what they've been telling themselves may not be as real as they thought. For example, we can often use words like 'everyone', 'all', 'nothing', 'every time' which are called 'nominalisations' in NLP. An example of a statement that someone may make could be 'Every time I do x this happens' or 'Everyone hates me'.

The use of the Meta Model aims to get specific but not by telling the person, simply by asking a question that will involve them having to think about their statement and come up with a more specific answer which in turn will affect their reality of the situation. To explain, the question could be "Has there ever been a time when you do x that it doesn't happen?", or "Is there one person that likes you?".

There were so many interesting conversations in the group and it was so insightful to hear things from a different perspective. There was another interesting technique that I enjoyed, it was called 'Perceptual Positions'. When we listened to the explanation and watched our tutor do a demonstration it seemed straight forward, but we were all slightly nervous about getting it wrong when we had to practise it ourselves.

We all had our training books with us, referring to them all the time and not wanting to get it wrong. Some would just wing it and do what they thought was right, of course we all made mistakes but that was the process of learning. I did struggle with trusting my gut instinct and felt I had to follow the book. I could feel myself getting stressed about not doing it right and not remembering what I had to do. I would always hope others would go first or that they would take the more difficult role in the exercise.

It certainly put us all through our paces and we were often in a situation where we had to come out of our comfort zones and just get on with it. Interacting and asking questions was a big part of the course, sharing ideas and having an interest in the interventions as they were called was a positive. Back to Perceptual Positions then, the exercise is about seeing a situation from a different perspective as the name suggests.

Self Help Tip:

There are 3 positions, you physically have 3 chairs and you move from one to the other and then back to the first chair.

The first chair is position 1, you see the situation/experience from your perspective, hearing, feeling everything.

Next you go to position 2 which is that of the other person involved, seeing, hearing and feeling the situation from their perspective.

Next is position 3, which is for the 'meta' person, so someone separate from the situation, they are viewing the situation like watching a TV screen. Seeing, hearing and feeling what is happening for all concerned. In this position, you can look at what tools and tips you would recommend to help the situation.

Lastly you return to position 1, your position and with all the learning you have from sitting in the other 2 seats you take that on board and see what you would do differently and take that into the future. Note: You can have more than 3 positions.

Sharing the experience with others over the nine non-consecutive weekends was a great format. It gave everyone time to process what they had learnt, time to practise and digest the information. I went around a lot of my friends and family and tested it out, they were very patient and I think some of them found it interesting.

I continued to meet up with those I'd connected with on the course, so we could practise and discuss what we had learnt. It was great to be with people who enjoyed talking about how people behave. I learned that it was acceptable to cry - showing emotion was not something that had been acceptable in our house. We always had to be strong and not show any sign of weakness. It got us nowhere.

It was such a relief - I felt totally supported and accepted, people were kind and friendly. At times, I found it difficult because I wasn't used to people showing affection and care. Not accustomed to crying in front of others, it took me a while to adjust. This has changed me dramatically because now I no longer see crying as a weakness but an acceptable emotion that is helpful to let out the hurt.

During the course, I learnt a lot about myself. Some things I already knew because I had been in and out of therapy for several years. But it opened my eyes up to assumptions I was making. Understanding the different techniques, and how that could enhance my life, was a real eye-opener.

I learnt more about acceptance and knowing that everyone has their own version of life and how they see it. It doesn't have to match mine and I can now accept that we are all different and no one is right or wrong.

I felt reassured to be different; it was fine to show emotion, it was natural.

It was great that I started to feel better about myself and value other people's opinions instead of being threatened by them. No one in the group was out to hurt me. They were all on their journey and the amount of knowledge in the room was incredible. I found it fascinating. I learned how to trust.

There were teachers, therapists and those who had businesses where NLP would be helpful. Others came for personal development like me. Everyone had their own views on things and we all learned and grew together.

There were mentors there to guide and support us, should anything happen they would be able to intervene; and carry on the interventions (techniques) that we were practising. They could always take us to a safe place either in our head or physically in the room. The mentors were previous NLP Practitioners from previous courses.

The interventions were varied. At times people dug deep into past hurts and history. Some dealt with light-hearted conflict; things that they wanted to achieve or change. It was different every time we met up but the connection between us all was strong. Everyone was supportive and offering to help where they could.

The NLP course was an important step in my journey, and opened my eyes to how we communicate with each other, and how quickly we can change things if we want to. At the end of the course we were all given a short piece of wood.

As the weeks passed by us we were getting closer and closer

to the end of the course, but also closer and closer to each other. We had a great bond and we pledged to keep in touch after the course. The last session involved us drawing on a piece of wood. On one side, we had to write on it what we wanted in our life and the other side was what we wanted to break through.

We then balanced our plank of wood across two breeze blocks. The 'Eye of the Tiger' track was played and we were poised over it with our hand on the board ready to 'smash through' our limitations to our aspirations. It was quite tricky to do! The trainer captured the moment on camera and the atmosphere in the room was euphoric.

For some reason, I couldn't manage to break my plank with my wrist so I had to do it with my foot. The tears were rolling down my face; I was so touched by what I'd put on the board and so caught up in the moment. I knew it was going to be hard to get the acceptance I sought, but I was determined.

It was a fantastic exercise to end the course. We had a celebratory catch-up after our training had finished, celebrating the passing of our exams. It wasn't just a course but a journey, I met some amazing people that shared intimate parts of their life and areas that troubled them. I felt exceptionally honoured to be in that situation and I too shared parts of me that I had never shared before so openly.

After I qualified as an NLP Practitioner, I went on to do the Master NLP Practitioner course, which covered more advanced techniques such as hypnosis in detail. I was very proud to have qualified as a Master Practitioner.

During the course, I met a woman who told me about Emotional Freedom Technique. She was running a course in it, with a qualification, and I thought it would be a good addition to my existing skills. Several of the people on the course intended to use their training to become counsellors, and I was no different. I wanted to help others as I'd helped myself - I knew I could be of use to people.

Having decided to take the EFT course, I found it to be amazing. The technique involves tapping your fingertips on the meridian points of the body whilst repeating a phrase about something concerning you. It releases the blocked negative energy in the body so it can clear. You feel better and let go of anything that was holding you back.

To say I absolutely loved it would be an understatement - it was easy to do and yet so effective. I was glad that I had my NLP training as you need to be careful when working with others.

When I passed, and received my certificate, I tested it out on anyone I could. I felt confident using it, and could see it was having great impact on others. I helped one friend deal with a needle phobia. On another occasion my sister felt sick whilst in hospital - I did some tapping and not long after the nausea passed. It was a blessing to have another tool, something else I could use to help myself and others.

It was important that I carried on my journey because I was determined to change myself. I didn't want to be like my parents, and I certainly didn't want to be the person others disliked or preferred not to be around. I wanted to have better relationships and I was determined to do all I could to improve that. Years had gone by from when I first started my therapy to doing the NLP and EFT courses and so I became so much better as the years went on.

My relationships started to improve and I started to make friends. They liked me, I couldn't believe it! I kept thinking to myself, they will tell me soon that there is a problem or stop talking to me but this never happened. People were saying positive things about me, about how kind and caring I was. Deep down I knew this but I didn't seem to deliver things well as a child and young person. Things were turning around for me and for the better.

My Board Break at NLP

A social catch up with my NLP friends

Chapter 21 - Liam

During the time of my NLP course I met up with some friends for a drink in the local pub just down the road from my flat. We were having our usual Sunday afternoon drinks and getting quite merry when I mentioned to my friends that I thought the guy at the bar was quite hot. He looked quite young but my friend wasn't exactly backwards in coming forwards so when we were at the bar ordering our drinks he asked him to come and join us for a drink after his shift.

It was a little embarrassing but secretly I was pleased and was feeling quite excited about it all. Later, in the afternoon he came to join us, his name was Liam and he sat next to us and started chatting. He seemed friendly enough but a little self-conscious, apparently bar staff weren't allowed to mix with the punters.

At this stage in my life I hadn't quite come to the realisation that I didn't need to save and rescue people anymore. We got chatting and I got the impression that he spoke quite negatively about himself, I instantly wanted to boost his confidence and said to stop saying things like that. We chatted for a good few hours, one minute we were chatting then the next kissing each other. It was fun and I felt very flattered as he was a lot younger than me.

The evening came to an end and he went off for a cigarette and didn't seem to come back to I headed home and said goodbye to my friends. It was a few weeks later that I went back to the pub, I wasn't sure if I would see him or not but I was really excited about the possibility. My heart with pumping and I had butterflies in my stomach, silly really but I did.

Walking into the pub with my friend I saw him behind the bar, we ordered our drinks and he was there serving someone. As the evening went on he approached me asking for my number and said he wondered where I went the first time we met, I explained I couldn't find him and went home. He said he looked out for me the following week so immediately I knew he was keen, I gave him my number and he asked if I was about once his shift finished around 11pm.

It was late but I gave him my address and he came over to my place after his shift finished. I was apprehensive and nervous but it was nice to see him, he was very good looking and I was really attracted to him. My only concern was his age and how mature he was. I knew where the night would probably lead but I was OK with it. We had sex and it was fun but he certainly had a lot to learn! I just had to decide if I wanted to be the one to teach him.

We started dating soon after and he would come over to my place quite a bit as he still lived at home with his Mum, her partner and sister. We would chat about all sorts of things and he came out with me and my friends to events and would pick me up if I'd been on a night out with girlfriends which was really kind.

The age gap for me was a problem and I felt that his immaturity was grinding on me after a while. From my NLP training I'd learnt to accept that other people weren't in the same place as me and that everyone's different. It was hard but I did learn that just because I liked or wanted something didn't mean someone else did.

Liam worked at the pub for a while after we got together but then left as he wasn't enjoying it anymore. One night he just literally walked out, which made me feel awkward because I was there that night with my sister and his boss was asking me where he'd gone and I didn't want to tell them anything of course. It was totally irresponsible on his part and didn't make me see his actions in a positive way.

The relationship only last a year or two because I realised that we were quite different. He didn't really enjoy the finer things of life like I do and I wanted to be able to go on holidays and go away for the weekends and be treated but he never really had any money. I felt that it was all on me, I also felt I became like a parent to him because of how he behaved.

It drove me mad that he was always late, not by 5, 10 or even 20 minutes but an hour or more. Sometimes he would go off to the corner shop for milk and not come back for hours.

He was really kind and I think he wanted to help everyone but would spread himself too thinly and end up disappointing everyone. He used to feel he couldn't get it right and everyone was moaning at him but he couldn't see that he caused it. His intention was good but it usually left people feeling let down.

Sometimes when we went out he didn't even have money for the car park. I did feel a lot of responsibility on my shoulders and I didn't want that in a boyfriend, I wasn't his mother after all. I wanted to be wined and dined and treated well, he wasn't that type of guy.

Whilst we persevered for a year or two on and off it just wasn't quite right. We could talk about it calmly which I was grateful of, I stopped getting angry and raising my voice after my NLP training. I learnt to communicate better, more calmly.

It was difficult at the time for me to get past the lateness and differences and I felt that the relationship wasn't really going to go anywhere. He didn't really have any ambitions and I wanted to be with someone that wanted similar things to me. Everything seemed to be interrupted, either he was getting phone calls from people wanting lifts here there and everywhere or he was nipping home to help his Mum and I was just in a different place to him mentally.

We decided to call it a day after realising it wasn't going to work. We still saw each other afterwards and just met up for sex every now and then but he moved on and had other relationships after me. It was certainly a learning curve, he did stand up for himself and make me see things from a different perspective which was good. I did see myself in him from years ago, always wanting to help people and doing too much and not having any time for myself. I'm not sure he's learnt his lessons yet, maybe one day.

Chapter 22 - Mindfulness

After completing my courses in 2009 early 2010, I wanted to set up as a therapist and help others. I invested time into getting my business up and running; and created my own website because I love IT and it was a great learning experience for me too. I had leaflets printed and business cards designed and prepared and started to get 'out there' and network so people knew who I was and how I could help them.

At the time, I was still working for the insurance company and doing this in my spare time. Work was exceptionally quiet and I was unhappy there as I had very little to do. I did tell my management team but not a lot changed so I made the most of the situation I was in and developed my business.

I had a few clients and ran a couple of free workshops on EFT to help people understand what it was and how it could help them. I felt so fulfilled that my learning was finally being put to good use; and it was noticeably helping others. Obviously, EFT wasn't for everyone but I got great feedback.

Whilst I loved doing it for whatever reason the business failed to thrive. I wasn't getting enough clients and felt frustrated. Possibly I didn't give it time to get going - all new businesses take a while to gain momentum - but I felt I was good at it and people were responding in a positive way. Eventually I folded the business. I was upset as I'd invested time into it but I knew it wasn't wasted. I had learnt a lot and it would be useful to me in the future.

It wasn't the right time for me, and everything happens for a reason. Once I watched a video called 'The Secret', about the law of attraction, thinking positively and putting out there what you want as a first step towards getting it from the universe. It can be challenging for some to grasp the concept but I have started thinking about and saying out loud what I want and the impact has been positive. If things haven't turned out the way I had hoped, it's because they weren't meant to for whatever reason.

The process helped give me focus and I learned where my passions lay. My full-time job was not fulfilling; and I was at a stage where I needed to think about what I wanted to do with my life. I certainly didn't want to stay where I was.

In 2012, I discovered something called Mindfulness and on learning more about it, decided it was something I needed to explore. The eight week course I took subsequently was to help with being present in the moment. I was becoming aware of some of my old anxieties returning at this point and thought mindfulness might help.

When I walked into the room it felt so welcoming. It was peaceful yet friendly and I loved the tone of the practitioner's voice. We learned different types of meditation throughout the course and had discussions about our daily practice and what distracted us whilst meditating. Often, we would have struggles in terms of 'doing it right', but soon learned that the beauty of mindfulness meditation is that there is no right or wrong way to do it. I found that very refreshing.

Our minds will always think about things; that is how the mind works, but it's down to us to bring our thoughts back to the present moment until the next time we get distracted. It was good that there were no rules, I was fed up of rules.

By this point in my self-development journey I found it easier to accept what I was and I stopped giving myself such a hard time. I understood that in life just as in mindfulness, there was no right way. It was a relief to know I could 'go with the flow' a little more.

I took each session as it came. If I fell asleep during one of the longer meditations I just enjoyed it for what it was. This was so far removed from the person I'd been. The intention behind the training is to develop a formal practice of meditation and for a while I did it religiously. It made me feel better; I would sit in my car before going into work and meditate. I felt set up for the day and calm. At times, I would take myself off into another room or space if I needed to think or calm down.

For some reason, as time went on, I lost the discipline to keep to a regular practice. The course encourages you to be mindful when you eat and do daily activities and I managed to do that when I was swimming or in the shower and sometimes when I was eating but not all the time. The main benefits come from meditating regularly and with intention. I wanted to do more but could not factor it into my day.

Self Help Tips:

Try having a short 5-minute meditation on your phone which you can access via You Tube or whatever is easy. I recommend Jon Kabat Zinn.

Where possible fit this into your day somewhere, whether it's in the car before you go into work, when you wake up in the morning. Again, the easier it is to fit in the more likely you are to do it.

I now attend the occasional meditation days and retreats. I love the sense of peace it gives me when life is hectic. Whilst I appreciate it isn't as committed as my mindfulness teacher would prefer, I've learnt to adapt it to me and my life.

Meditation also helped my anxiety and my need for control. All the problems that plagued me whilst I was growing up seem to be drifting away or lessening as I get older.

Shortly after finishing my meditation course I was inspired to take it further and I booked myself onto a meditation retreat in Devon. This was to be my first ever trip away by myself. I kept telling everyone I was going away on holiday. Little did I know that this was no holiday, it was a major step outside of my comfort zone and I was in for a shock!

Chapter 23 – Time for a change

In 2011, after 12 years doing IT purchasing and training I moved into a new role at work. I fancied a change so I applied for a role in the project management office. It involved helping the project managers with the reporting for their projects and general support. I was based in the Poole office whilst my manager and colleague were based in the Romford IT department.

It was a steep learning curve as all the roles had been at work but I enjoy a challenge and did it to the best of my ability. I had to learn more about running projects what all the acronyms meant which was interesting and the finance side to ensure the projects stayed in budget. We would have a weekly call and I needed to keep notes about where we were with each of the projects and update it in each of the project notes and then this information was used for reports for the management team.

My colleague worked in Romford and she only worked part-time, she had been doing the job a while and I seemed to pick it up quickly and was able to make some helpful time saving changes which I felt good about. I found the work fairly straight forward but it wasn't exactly something I was passionate about and this was to be my final role at the insurance company.

171

The role involved me going up and down to Romford to be with the rest of my team which was OK, it was nice to feel part of a team. When my manager changed half way through my role I had to travel to our London office which is where he was based. The city was a bit hectic for me and I didn't enjoy the stress of having to get from A to B on the train and then tube to the office. Sometimes I felt anxious that I would miss the train and not make it in time for meetings but I was always fine.

The role was quite interesting and did challenge me, I was learning more about project management and understanding the connection between IT and the businesses within our group. I was still struggling with my professional relationships at the time. Generally I didn't have a can do attitude and was inflexible to people's requests. I was the same in my training role and I struggled to change it.

As with most of my roles once I had a good understanding of what I was doing and making things more efficient where I could, I got bored. I found days and periods of time that would stand still because I had little to keep me occupied.

It's interesting how long you can stay in a situation for that is uncomfortable or not making you feel good. I should have left my job long before I did, but having the security of a job kept me there. My mind would tell me I wouldn't financially cope without it, that I wouldn't be able to find another role in the area that paid as well.

Our minds are so good at keeping us stuck, stuck in the difficulties and stresses of life. What's controlling us are our thoughts and that is what we need to look at if we don't want to be held hostage in our own lives. Telling ourselves it will be OK and getting evidence to prove it, knowledge is power so finding out how easy or difficult it is to do something e.g. leave a job may not be as bad as we are telling ourselves.

Maybe if I took a step to contact agencies or did more serious job hunting it would have raised my confidence levels. I do accept that if you aren't in the right place and things aren't bad enough we often won't do anything to help ourselves. I think staying where I was kept me nicely in my comfort zone.

Chapter 24 – The Retreat

During my role in the projects team of March 2012, I decided to take a holiday as I naively saw it. The Barn retreat had been recommended to me by my meditation teacher and I thought it sounded interesting and a good thing to do soon after my course. I arrived at The Barn in Devon, it was a beautiful place in the middle of nowhere with a narrow lane to get to the house. As I approached the entrance, I carefully drove the car up the narrow track which was windy and with some sharp turns. I parked up in the car park and made my way to the front door. There was no response to my knocking and I felt a little uncomfortable. No one was around. I found the whole experience daunting and felt extremely nervous. This was just because I was in a new place and didn't know what to expect, I started to panic.

Finally, someone arrived, but it wasn't the people that ran the retreat. It was some of the other people staying there. We got chatting and made a drink, and eventually the people that worked there came in and introduced themselves as the retreat co-ordinators.

They showed us around the rooms in the house and we were asked to choose a room which was great as no one else had arrived at that time. I picked a room that overlooked the car park and had beautiful views of the countryside. I went out to the car to get my bags and unpack so I could feel a bit more settled. It was interesting sitting down in the lounge and watching others arrive and talking to them about where they had come from and what previous experience they had of meditation.

The feel of the house was calming but I still felt apprehensive. Once everyone had arrived we gathered for an initial introduction and were given the rules of the house - no mobile phones, no talking on Wednesdays or after 9pm at night until 8am the next day. I accepted not talking (I know that will surprise my friends and family!); I lived on my own so I had moments of silence when I wasn't keeping busy.

We were allocated chores. Part of staying at the retreat involved helping on the land and in the house which seemed fair as the cost of the week was reasonable. It also added to the experience of the meditation; doing 'mindful' work, taking your time and being present in the tasks you were doing. I'm not sure I grasped the concept then as much as I have now, but I did my best at the time.

We had a strict schedule. There were four meditations a day and the first one was at 7am. I like structure so this was fine, although I was not that excited about the early starts. We went in for our first morning meditation and we were all sat around in a circle, in a room with big glass panes from floor to ceiling which overlooked the garden. The room was serene and had maroon colour round meditation cushions, blankets and pillows so we had enough to be comfortable. Some people did bring their own cushions and mats.

Once everyone got settled the session began, we were guided through the meditation which lasted about an hour.

After our morning meditation, we did chores and sat down to breakfast. It was mainly a vegan menu but at times I managed to get away with baking some cakes or naughty biscuits. I tried some porridge with golden syrup for sweetness, which I got used to and had for the duration of my stay.

The rest of the morning was ours to do as we wished. There was a beautiful library where you could relax and watch the day go by or read if you wanted to. I did some mindful work in the garden and was given the task of chopping up the branches using a shredder. It was quite vicious but I enjoyed it. It was quite therapeutic! Others were chopping wood; some were gardening, cleaning, cooking and generally helping. There was a sense of community and camaraderie which I liked because it gives me a feeling that everyone is supporting each other, with the same goals and intentions. I spoke to a few of the other people on the retreat but I found it hard - at our discussion times I shared that I was feeling unsafe because it was a new environment for me.

The leader took me aside and we discussed my discomfort. I felt better after telling him how I felt and as the week continued I started to feel much more comfortable. I became more aware that I found new situations difficult – I was uncomfortable and out of my comfort zone, and felt scared.

Self Help Tips:

If you suffer with anxiety and feel uncomfortable with the unknown, I'd recommend doing your research and maybe even speaking to people before you do things to get some reassurance. Find out the information you need to make you feel more safe and comfortable.

This of course links to my anxiety – I wasn't aware of the connection at the time. The unknown is something I lived with my whole life at home; we couldn't predict what was going to happen so I felt perpetually anxious. That is why I need and want control; so, that I feel security. I realise now after all the years of self-development that I wasn't in control of anything but in my head that is how it felt. This was throughout my life not just in one area.

Insider Tip:

An alcoholic home is extremely unpredictable and you are forever living on eggshells, not knowing the mood of the drinker at any one time. With that in mind you can become quite anxious and uncertainty is something you must live with but it's not easy.

I enjoyed my time at The Barn. I had time to think and be in the moment and peaceful. It was good to be mindful and start noticing the small things; the colour of the grass, and the sound of the birds. All the things we take for granted each day - we forget to look at and take in our surroundings, because it is there all the time. I feel now that I'm much more aware of taking in my environment. I also feel more gratitude and appreciation.

Self Help Tips:

I highly recommend a gratitude journal and starting to pay attention to things around you that you may otherwise take for granted.

Just arriving at The Barn Retreat, Sharpham

The view from my bedroom

Beautiful view from my walk at The Barn

The Greenhouse, lots of vegetables for dinner

Chapter 25 – Al-Anon

In September 2012, I was given a book, one that I'd read a few years previously. On re-reading it, the effect was different. The book, 'Women Who Love Too Much', is about co-dependency. Co-dependency is about having too much emotional or psychological reliance on another person, usually found in those with an addiction.

Reading it was like having a proper diagnosis. It talked about all the struggles in my life – it could have been about me! The relief was unbelievable and a huge weight was lifted from my shoulders. There were stories from other people, stories that I could relate to, from people that had grown up in an alcoholic home or lived with an alcoholic. The similarity of their behaviour was astounding.

It was interesting why the book had such an effect the second time, why didn't I feel like that after reading before?

It is true that we must be in the right state of mind to make any kind of change work. We can't make ourselves see things about ourselves until we are ready! After finishing the book, I decided to do exactly what it suggested - go to an Al-Anon group. Apparently, there I would find like-minded people offering support.

I thought it was a little over the top. My father had died when

I was nearly twenty-one, I was no longer living with the alcoholism; it was all years ago - what good could it do me now?

How wrong I was!

It took a lot for me to muster up the courage to walk through the doors of that first meeting. I had no idea why I was finding it so hard – after all I was no stranger to self-development and facing my issues. But this was different and the fear was there – a mixture of tension, apprehension and nerves. There were about eight people in the room, all friendly and welcoming. They gave me an envelope and said there would be time at the end for questions - if I wanted to speak I could, but there was no pressure to do so.

There is always a standard format to Al-Anon meetings. Everyone is welcomed then they read out the twelve 'steps', which are also used by Alcoholics Anonymous (AA). They also read the twelve 'traditions', and people could then share about their week.

This sharing varied from person to person. For some it was about the stresses and strains of living with an alcoholic. For others, it was about challenges and how they were coping.

In the group people don't interrupt or ask questions, they just listen to you and thank you once you have finished. Everyone has a chance to speak. Then someone reads something of interest and others share their thoughts or talk about something on their mind.

Of course, I had a lot of questions! I had no idea how it worked and what was going on. I like structure and knowing as much as I can so I feel in control. This was out of my comfort zone - I felt awkward and nervous. However, this feeling did not last for long and I began to feel more comfortable with time - everything was very non-judgemental, and that was refreshing.

In the end, I attended Al-Anon for about a year. I went to one area meeting and it was interesting to see how Al-Anon works at a higher level, and to meet new people. One person was my sponsor - recommended when working through your problems. She had been part of Al-Anon for over 20 years; and her opinions and beliefs were in line with my own.

Having a sponsor was amazing. I felt that this was the support and understanding that I'd been searching for my whole life. Someone was there for me no matter what and understood where I was coming from - because she had been there herself. We were so similar! I could learn from her experience of living with an alcoholic and, most importantly, see which behaviours no longer served her in a positive way.

The Al-Anon programme is there to help you to recover *yourself* and help you realise what behaviours, good and bad, you have learned from living with/being with an alcoholic. I thought that the problem was my Dad's - I wasn't the one that was sick. But Al-Anon opened my eyes, it was a smack in the face to read the courage to change book, and after going to a few meetings, I realised I was in a worse state than I thought. In my opinion I was doing well (to be fair I have improved a lot over the years) but I was still in denial about a lot of things. I mean how can you know you are in denial if you are in denial?!

After a time, I realised how sick I was but became more open to accepting and verbalising things about myself. The term 'insane' and 'insanity' are used at Al-Anon and that has been difficult too. But I've learnt to accept that at times my behaviour *has* been 'insane'. But I'm not my behaviour, and I'm not an insane person. It's just that some of my behaviour over the years has fit the word. I'm beginning to understand why this is.

I'm like a lot of others in Al-Anon. We want quick fixes, but the programme doesn't work like that. It takes a long time to recover from things that have been learnt and ingrained in our behaviour for years, but Al-Anon was the start of me being awake to myself. **This was one of the biggest turning points in my life.**

I loved the support that was available, and listening to and learning from others. I'd been searching for understanding for so many years and the group gave me a fulfilment that I'd never experienced in the past. It gave me the strength to know I can cope with life, that I'd be ok, and to write this book.

Chapter 26 – Self Development Journey

Now is a good time to review my development so far and how I feel I've changed over the years. I regularly reflect on my life and how far I've come, because it's important to get perspective. Making the decision to change was an obvious one to me but I appreciate it isn't an easy one for most, I just knew things had to be better.

One of the biggest learnings was that for any change to work you must *want* it. Initially you may not have complete awareness, you just know something isn't right. Either you are unhappy or something isn't working well in your life and you want it to be different in a positive way. Initially I wasn't sure what it would involve, but I was determined, so I went for it.

To give an example, I knew I was being aggressive to people and I knew that because people told me and I could feel it myself after a while and after I realised what I had been doing, I chose to do something about it because it was affecting my life and my relationships specifically. I wanted to have better relationships and I knew it would require commitment and effort but I was prepared to invest in it because it was important enough to me.

Just after I finished my EFT course in 2010 I went to a Louise Hay conference and read some of her books. She inspired me to make positive changes in my life. Hay had been through tough times and got through it with the use of positive affirmations and a better diet; improving her mental wellbeing through positive thinking, facing her fears and understanding the connections between thoughts and illness.

I also read a fabulous book called 'Feel the Fear and Do It Anyway' by Susan Jeffers. This book was an inspiration. I loved the way Jeffers wrote and I found the information in the book practical and helpful to me at a time when I needed it.

I've read so many books over the years, several to do with living with alcoholics. I now understand more about the type of habits that are developed by children of alcoholics and how they affected me. Whilst I admit I did go a little 'mad', they taught me an awful lot. I'm always learning new things which I think is important - I like to stimulate my brain by learning and understanding more about myself.

'Change Work' (which is what it is called) is not always easy and takes commitment and dedication. If you want to be able to be different or face something that is holding you back, then I can only say - go for it! It has worked for me in the most amazing way and this book explains the techniques I've used which you can also try if you want to live a calmer, easier and more fulfilling life.

Self Help Tips:

- Reflect on your current repetitive situations and behaviours and decide if it is something you want to address
- Once you have decided and accepted that you want to change, consider what route you wish to take e.g. therapy, self-help books, courses, alternative therapies etc. (you may need to consider costs and options – some therapy is available free through the NHS)
- Take one step forward to start the process e.g. buy the book, book an appointment, attend an event
- Be patient with yourself, you have been this way for years so know it will take time for changes to happen
- Reflect on your chosen method to see how it is helping you, you may decide to do a few in parallel e.g. therapy and self-help books
- Do what you can to help yourself and be pro-active. Change only happens if you make it so

My family and friends have seen me transform from an aggressive, nasty and quite frankly horrible person at times to a caring, loving, kind and fun person to be around. I'd always had a good sense of humour but I think it got lost somewhere along the way, that can happen when you live with an alcoholic I took everything so seriously.

> **Insider Tips:**
>
> It is quite common in children of alcoholics that they become overly responsible and fun is eliminated from the home. Often, they must help in the home because the drinker is absent, both mentally and physically.

When I hear, people say they can't change, I know that isn't technically true. People may say that because they don't *want* to change. I know it can be done because I'm living, breathing proof of it. Everyone has choices, either to choose to change or accept its stagnation.

My self-awareness over the years has increased dramatically. I had no idea about some of my faults as I would call them, which basically meant my behaviours but that is how I saw it. I wasn't perfect and I saw them as negative things rather than aspects of me. As I've gradually developed a greater awareness of myself.

Acceptance isn't something with which I've been familiar over time. I had to accept that I'm an opinionated, outspoken person but never wanted to be aggressive and rude; so, I did something about it. I also wanted to feel better about myself and have better relationships so I worked on that and have successfully turned it around.

My NLP course enabled me to look at things in a completely different way, understand that everyone comes from their own 'map of the world' as they understood it. They all have their own experiences, behaviours and learning and I would have made judgements and assumptions based on my own beliefs which weren't true for others. I would apply my own thoughts and feelings to how others behaved without any idea of what they had been through and empathy about why they did the things they did. With the flexibility, I learnt and understood that others didn't think like me, once I got my head around that I could be more accepting.

My family and friends have been a great support to me. They have kept me going with always an ear to listen and someone to talk to. I realised as the years went on how hard it must have been for them when I was changing. They had to adjust to the new me.

This has taken time to settle but I know they prefer the person I am now to the person I use to be! I have close relationships with my Mum and sister and we see each other regularly. We still have our differences, especially my Mum and I but nowhere near the same degree that they were 10-15 years ago.

Chapter 27 – Redundancy Changed My Life

After working 14 years for the insurance company I was made redundant, I was initially shocked at the news but relieved at the same time because I wasn't enjoying it and hadn't been for several years. It was the push I needed and people often say it's the best thing that can happen. I do believe that these things can then provide opportunities and allow us to do more of what we really want to do. I was lucky enough to get redundancy pay which allowed me a little bit of a buffer until I found a new job which wasn't until 3 months later.

The last year of my job there was probably one of the most challenging of my work life so far. I felt totally useless and demotivated, I told my boss I didn't have much work to do, I would ask others at work if they had anything they wanted help with but there was never really enough to fill an eight hour day. This went on for about a year and the frustration I felt was immense. I felt guilt at the same time that I was doing hardly any work but then I did all I could to raise the issue.

Obviously at that time I had no idea I was going to be made redundant, so maybe that was part of their strategy, not to give me work in the hope I would leave so they wouldn't have to pay me redundancy pay. Whilst I had all this time to myself I started setting up my own business to do the therapy I wanted to offer. I set up a website and did a lot of research and anything and everything I could think of that would help me start up. It was quite good to have the time to do it but again I did feel guilty that I was doing my own thing in work time, but no one seemed to care.

The day came when I found out a lot of the IT department in Poole were going to be made redundant. We were called into the boardroom at work and there was a big announcement from Mark via a conference call. He explained that there were cuts and the usual load of rubbish about costs and finances. We all left the room with different feelings, views and opinions.

There was a lot of talk within the team as well as speculation, over a few months it became known that more of us were being made redundant and that included me. There was a strict process and someone had to be nominated as a spokesperson and they would represent us all to ensure everything was fair. It was a difficult time for everyone but I was OK about it, they did send mixed messages about my role. Initially I wasn't being made redundant then I was, then I could apply for my role but it would be based in Romford.

It was quite frustrating and some people were getting quite annoyed about how they dealt with it but it was all going to happen whatever, so I just accepted it in the end and was quite surprised by my reaction. I wasn't feeling anxious or worried I felt free and that this was all happening for the right reasons, I knew I wasn't happy and being forced to leave was probably the best thing.

In February 2013, three months after we found out about the redundancies, I left the company with a lot of the others, although we all left at slightly different times. Some got jobs and some didn't but had things in the pipeline. I had no idea what I was going to do although my dream was to have my own business.

Thankfully I got myself a nice redundancy package which was nice, but I had been there for about 14 years. No leaving gift and no thank you for all your hard work but that was to be expected.

A month after being made redundant in March 2013 I decided to book a real holiday in Devon by myself for a week. I realised I had to start small and pluck up the courage to go away on my own building new memories that would enable me to do it again.

I found this great barn conversion to stay in and I had it all to myself. It was beautifully decorated and I could do all my own cooking. As I drove up the very long driveway I parked in front of my entrance (there were two other places next door that were rented out). I went inside as the owners left it open for me, as I walked inside I was greeted by a beautiful lounge, Kitchen/diner. There was a large Inglenook fireplace to my right and the sofa placed directly in front of it. Straight ahead was a window slightly off to the right and then to the left was the kitchen and dining table. The window next to the table overlooked the back garden which was like a field.

The kitchen was modern and the walls were cream with lovely furnishings. It felt very cosy and on the dining table they had left me a note to welcome me with a scone, butter and jam to enjoy which was placed under a netted cover to keep the flies away.

So much thought had gone into it and I truly appreciated the effort.

As I walked between the kitchen and the dinner table there was a doorway to the bedroom. It was lovely, not too big but enough for a double bed and to the right was a window overlooking the back garden and to the left was a door to the en-suite bathroom. I loved it!

As well as my clothes and food, I took my sewing machine because I wanted to make some clothes and I thought it would give me something to do whilst I was away. I hadn't grasped the 'total relaxation' idea at that stage! I was still used to filling my time with 'doing' things because relaxing seemed like a waste of time if I wasn't being productive.

My first night was very nice and I had a good night's sleep, I made myself some breakfast and decided to visit the local area. I was near Honiton in Devon and it was nice and quaint.

During my time at the barn I visited local towns and went shopping in Exeter; I found a local swimming pool and managed to get in a swim or two during my stay. I did feel very grateful for the pool at home because when I compared the price and the facilities we got a better deal. It made me reflect on what we take for granted, how lucky I was with the pool I swam in at home compared to the one I went to. There was flooding in the changing area and very small benches to put your clothes on to get ready and the hairdryers were quite old.

I didn't go out at night because I didn't feel I needed to and I didn't have anyone to go out with anyway. I spent the days out and about, going for walks and enjoying myself so I was happy to relax in the evening.

Whilst I was there I had what I can only describe as *a 'light bulb' moment. It was another one of those points in my life where I had a moment of intense awareness.* I looked at myself in the mirror and saw the person looking back at me and whilst I recognised the face, in the strangest way I didn't recognise the person at all.

Saying clearly to myself "I'm not who I thought I was at all". I just looked at myself and stood in complete shock as I saw somebody new. It was the strangest feeling but things just began to click into place. I realised that I had been putting on a front for people - maybe even for myself.

If I'm honest I was quite taken back, I felt scared and confused about what I had believed to this point. I realised I hadn't been as open as I thought with people, well at least not in an authentic way. I was still telling people what I thought they wanted to hear and probably myself. I began to realise that there was another person deep inside that I hadn't been sharing with others. I'd been keeping her close to my heart and behind a wall and that felt false to me.

I felt dazed and overwhelmed by this discovery. Thankfully I was due to return home, although I knew I would miss the place I was staying in because it was so beautifully calm and inviting. It provided me with the environment I needed to have my revelation, safe, structured and devoid of pressure. No wonder my true self felt it was OK to come out at last.

Self Help Tips:

If you have something you would like to do but it seems far too daunting here are my suggestions:

Small steps are best, going from nothing to something big can be scary.

Break down the large task into chunks which will make them much more manageable. Do that however you like, mind maps, drawing pictures, writing lists.

Prioritise your list in terms of what you think needs to be done first, based on urgency/importance

Start with the first task and if you need help, ask for it – no man is an island – don't assume others will think you are a burden or assume they won't have time or anything else your mind tells you

Keep going – pat yourself on the back after each one – keep going (tell your mind "thanks I hear you" every time it starts to sabotage you with things like "you can't do that" etc)

Celebrate once you have finished – YOU DID IT

Chapter 28 - One Step Forward, One Step Back

I signed on at the job centre and applied for several jobs and eventually I was interviewed and offered a role working on a tourism project based at Bournemouth University three months after my redundancy.

The relief of getting that job was amazing and once I knew I had secured a role I could relax. Honestly, I was frustrated at myself because it would have been great to have that hindsight and to know it would all work out so I could have really enjoyed the previous 3 months that I had off. Trusting my gut instinct was growing with time, but when it comes to financial matters I was still a little apprehensive which I think is quite normal. I was still single so I didn't really have anyone financially to help support me.

The job was straight forward and because it was a new project it was exciting to get stuck into something that needed setting up. I liked the variety and challenge of the role but after a few weeks it became obvious that the role wasn't enough for me. I wasn't really learning that much just using the skills I was fortunate to accumulate from my last job. It turned out that there was another opening for a trainer. I was keen to apply because I had previously done training in my last position and I enjoyed it.

I spent a long time doubting myself and wondering if I was capable and had the expertise as it was in an industry I wasn't as familiar with as I'd have liked.

Eventually after support and persuasion from my friends and family I applied or the job. I can remember the moment I was informed that I got it. I was so happy, I literally couldn't believe I'd done it. What a great example of just going with something and waiting to see what happens, you just never know and you should always aim higher than you think.

The job was only on a two-year contract and it was going to be reviewed on an ongoing basis due to funding. I had never worked in the public sector before and I must say I never would again.

When I got the job, I knew I was due to have some surgery on my foot, so I informed my employer. I'd had an accident the previous year when I went to Kos with my Mum and Simon – I went to show Mum a lovely rock pool area that I had found and one minute I was saying how lovely and clear the water was and the next I had slipped on the rocks and I fell in, still holding onto my camera in one hand I used the other to stop myself before reaching the other side of the rocks.

I was just screaming in pain and my Mum was just laughing uncontrollably. I suppose it looked funny from her viewpoint. I was a bit shocked and couldn't believe that I hadn't smashed up my camera. I couldn't really move very easily so Mum had to come and help me.

Mum and Simon both had one of my arms over their shoulders and we started walking or should I say hopping on my part back to the sunbeds where Simon was enjoying the heat and relaxing. The ground we were walking on was just grey large rocks, some rounded but some more jagged and uneven. When we finally reached Simon I sat down on the sunbed under the umbrella, the heat was making it unbearable and I was getting more agitated because the pain started kicking in.

Mum suggested sitting with my foot in the sea water which I did for a time and it did ease the pain a bit. Eventually we had to get back to the hotel to see if I could get it looked at. The hotel were very good and I sat near the bar area and the barman came and poured Ouzo or something on it. To say it had a sting effect was an understatement, my toe was getting black and my foot was swelling up. Thankfully the hotel had some crutches which totally saved my life. We were due to leave the next day so it could have been a lot worse.

Once I got back home to the UK I went to the doctor and got it all checked out and it was OK after some treatment. Some months later I discovered I'd developed 'Morton's Neuroma' - a lump on the nerve. I was having trouble walking as it was like walking on a rock so after visiting the podiatrist and discussing my options I decided to have surgery to remove it. At the time, I also had a bunion on the same foot and so the podiatrist suggested we could do it at the same time, so that's what we did.

The podiatrist explained the process and I agreed to have the surgery done under local anaesthetic. Now anyone that knows about this operation will know that was probably not my best decision! That said, I was taking the advice of a professional who assured me that it would just be a couple of injections in my foot. What was there to worry about?

Thankfully I never researched bunion surgery or anything to do with what I was having done, which was just as well because I'm not sure I would have gone through with it. As I said, I had only just started the job at the University but they understood. I thought I would only be off for a couple of weeks.

Some weeks after the initial decision for surgery it was time for the operation. Daisy drove me to the hospital with Mum which was nice, I wasn't able to go alone of course. I was quite ignorant about what the procedure entailed. The doctor arrived and explained what was going to happen; he prepared me for the injections. I was lying there on the hospital bed with Daisy to my right and Mum to my left and as soon as Mum saw the needles she was out of there, her and needles don't go.

Daisy on the other hand loves the blood and gore so she was quite happy to sit and watch. At one point Daisy said, "Your foot looks like a pin cushion!". I must have had about fourteen injections all over my foot; it was the most excruciating pain I had ever experienced. I realised at that point I should have opted for the general anaesthetic, I was in so much pain.

Shortly after I headed into the operating theatre and as they started working on me I could still feel my foot. They had to give me *more* injections, I felt them tugging at my nerve and it was so scary but the nurses were there to reassure me. They talked to me so I was distracted but hearing the drills and feeling tugging at my foot was not the best experience of my life. I felt so alone and bewildered in the operating theatre but as soon as it was all over the relief set in. Daisy and Mum took me home and got me settled in, I couldn't really do a lot so Mum stayed with me for a few nights.

Friends did pop over and see me when they could and bring lovely food and treats for me, I was very well looked after which was very much appreciated. It was some time after the operation that I realised how traumatised I was from the experience. It knocked me for six and I did get quite emotional at the time when I realised how upset I was. It felt like a total invasion of my body, does that make sense? I wasn't use to going into hospital and I was very grateful for that. The realisation just came upon me and I was so shocked that I got so upset.

The overwhelm of feelings was something I was getting used to but it did still take me by surprise. I'm just so use to getting on with things and not feeling, that when it happens it takes me back a bit.

This whole experience had a major impact on me. Not just because of the physical operation and rehabilitation (which took five weeks!) but the mental changes that occurred when I couldn't walk. I couldn't drive for a few weeks and it was difficult to get around. I felt totally helpless and reliant on Mum for support. I'm so independent so being in a situation where I was forced to give that up was challenging, I hated not being able to get on with my life.

Whilst friends and family did pop in, I spent a lot of time on my own. Daisy had the boys to look after but she did what she could to help out.

The trouble was I still struggled with my own company. Whilst I lived on my own and familiar with periods of silence, being at home for such a long time in one go was difficult to handle. Normally I would arrange to do something each evening and in any spare time I had because I didn't want to be alone and potentially face my own issues.

During the five weeks, I had off work I spent a lot of time watching TV series, I watched 'Breaking Bad' and 204 episodes of '24'. I was someone that never really watched TV so it was quite intense, if you have ever been addicted to a TV series I'm sure you'll relate if you watched any back to back. It's so addictive, isn't it? I think I even started dreaming about it because I was watching it so intensely.

Time at home after the surgery on my foot forced me to face my fears about being alone; and my mind-set changed completely. Eventually I came to realise that I liked being on my own and no longer felt the need to fill my diary with appointments.

It's funny how we must be forced into situations to change and grow. This happened for the best and I believe that is the same as what happened with my redundancy, I was forced into the situation but it was the best thing for me.

What a break through!

Beautiful flowers from my work colleagues

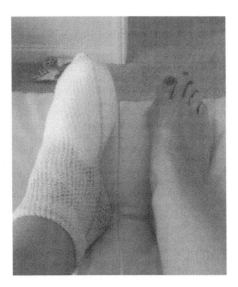

My poorly foot

Time to Reflect

So many changes and so much awareness happened in the time I left work. I loved the fact I was forced into a change in job and in a sense made to enjoy my own company when I had my surgery because I'm not sure I would have changed those things off my own back.

Those situations even though they were very difficult meant that I had to deal with it or be swallowed up by it. A lot of people I know have been prescribed anti-depressants and I was offered them by my doctor when I was struggling but I refused because I generally don't like taking tablets and I had a fear that I'd get addicted to them. I also wanted to handle it by myself and not rely on them, I know they can save people's lives but I do feel the doctors don't always have a plan to get people off them.

To say I didn't have moments where I felt sorry for myself would be a lie, of course I did. It was totally shit at times and I hated it, I would talk to friends and family about my life a lot which was of course a contrast to what I was taught growing up. I think I did a 180 degree shift and did an all or nothing move from not talking to talking too much about things.

Most of the time I was going over and over the same things because my mind was so full of worries and concerns. One of the best tips my Mum shared with me (which of course I ignored) was this:

WRITE IT DOWN! GET IT OUT OF YOUR HEAD

Oh how right she was (that'll make her smile to read). It's true and I've heard it many times since from therapists, self-help books and the like. Once it's out of your head your mind is clear and you can think about it more clearly, or not at all.

When the realisation of what you've been doing that has been hindering you finally hits you, it's the best thing in the world. It's what you do with it then that matters.

Chapter 29 – Singing

If my life is generally good, and I'm happy, then things don't annoy me quite so much. I'm sure others have been in a situation where something someone has done or said has affected them badly. The more I think about it, the worse it gets. Then other small things become an issue, or frustrating, and so it goes on. It isn't to do with the other things it's about the first event that started you off.

Thankfully I'm accepting myself more and more. That has taken me fifteen years so far! So, when others find me frustrating or difficult, I have more confidence knowing that is their issue, not mine; and I can accept that now. This works the other way too. When I find others frustrating or I get angry, there is usually some message for *me* in there. If I find it, then I can look at what it was that was making me feel that way. Having that awareness is great for personal growth.

Over the years, I've had some great friendships but when they stopped working I decided to move on. I was probably not in a great place; or one that didn't fit with them at the time; so, I let go.

I'm the sort of person that needs to have closure; and because of my upbringing uncertainty doesn't sit well with me. I don't cope well with the unknown - although I'm better now than I used to. I like to know where I stand and that need is greater than my fear of confrontation with people.

It's my preference to get things out in the open, talk about them and resolve them where possible. Or, at the very least, agree a way forward because we all have different views, wants and needs and sometimes a compromise needs to be reached. (See my self-help tips on the next page).

For example, when I decided to join a choir I was worried. I'd never done anything like that before; I was apprehensive about the other people and whether they would like me or not. I still have insecurities now and accept that they are old patterns and habits of thinking. This fear is what I felt when I was a child; it isn't relevant anymore. People aren't always going to like me but that is fine.

The choir was certainly a long time coming. For years, I'd been singing in the shower, at home and to Daisy (because she loved it!) but I never did anything with my natural ability. I was singing in the car with a friend of mine and he said I should join a choir. I thought I should have singing lessons first to see if my voice was good enough so I started looking for a teacher.

I started having regular lessons with a teacher and we got on well. My anxiety was an issue - I was concerned about singing in front of someone I didn't know. What if she laughs and I'm humiliated? What if I sound awful and she tells me? Will I cope with the criticism?

Self Help Tips:

- Reflect on difficult situations/conversations with people that have affected you negatively
- In your reflection, note down exactly what it was that caused you to feel the way you felt. For example: x was late, x said y, x disrespected me, x forgot to let me know about...
- Being as open, honest and flexible as you can be – look at what you have written to see if there is some aspect of that in you that you struggle with. It may not be a direct connection but if you felt someone was being disrespectful, are you being disrespectful to yourself? Do you disrespect others? Someone may be late but it isn't about lateness it is probably about disrespect for example
- You may find that difficult but the more you do it the more awareness you are raising and the easy it will become to spot it in the future
- Choose whichever way suits you to deal with this in the future. I love inner child work, that involves you talking to the little you and reassuring them and understanding what they want because most of our current challenges relate to something historical! – I highly recommend a book called 'Healing the Child Within' by Charles Whitfield

I was used to being criticised by my father; but it still hurt. Every new experience I had led me to learn more about my feelings; understanding more about me and what upset me; what made me anxious and what made me happy or sad.

So, I continued with the lessons and I opened up more and more as time went on. I was delighted when my teacher asked me to join her choir, and I said yes immediately - I wanted to do something with my singing and not just sing at home or in the car. She was mad as a hatter but I really liked her, she was very holistic and did lots of wellbeing things like sound baths (which is using sound bowls and some percussion instruments to bathe you in the lovely sounds in order to feel better and deal with negative emotions and troubles). She also did chakra work which was really relaxing.

Soon I was attending the group each week and although initially some of the group weren't as friendly as others (it is always hard to come into something when relationships are already established), I kept going.

Of course, I found things difficult at times - things weren't as structured as I liked them, so I felt there was a lack of focus. We seemed to move from one song to the next without learning one properly; and I wanted to get each one perfect. I didn't read music but I just practised the recordings I would take so I could learn at home.

Being part of a group of like-minded people was great, it was nice to finally do something with my voice. I loved learning and it was fun too. Some of the songs weren't my favourites but I was just glad for the opportunity. After a while my singing teacher wanted to start getting things a little more structured and get more gigs. I volunteered to help her run things and do the admin side of the choir, she was thrilled and we would meet every now and then to discuss how to take things forward.

We had some meetings and got ideas from the rest of the group which I thought was really helpful, inevitably there were some disagreements but also understanding. Knowing how difficult certain parts were for some people and being open allowed people to have a bit more empathy. Sometimes it got boring when you had to stand around and wait for people to get their part right.

My singing teacher meant well but she wasn't business minded and I think she ping ponged between wanting to take it forward and progress and not wanting it to be too serious.

As time progressed we did local performances, supported a band called 'The Worry Dolls' which was great, performed at events and Christmas gigs which were exciting and boosted my confidence.

It became apparent that after a while some people in the group practised more than others and a few wanted different things from the choir. Some just wanted to have fun and sing; whilst others wanted to progress. After considering what I wanted, I decided to leave. I wasn't enjoying the type of music; the lack of structure was hard for me and at the time I was planning to go travelling to America for three months so the timing seemed right.

It wasn't to be the last of my singing.

Chapter 30 – Experience of My Life

In June 2014, I decided to go travelling. It was something I'd wanted to do for a long time, talked about before but never gone through with it for one reason or another. I decided to go to America for three months. I was excited because I knew it was going to be an amazing journey. I love America and my gut just told me that it was the right thing to do.

There was a lot of thought that went into the planning of the trip, how much it would cost, where I would stay, what I would see and do. The list was endless. I was on a fixed contract at work at the time, which would have ended just before I wanted to go, the following February.

Something like this is a big thing for anyone and I was finally doing it. Now I feel I need to stress here that this was a MASSIVE step for me, totally out of my comfort zone BUT I wanted it more than anything. It felt right and I knew I could do it. I was in a much better place after my Devon trip. I had already started doing more on my own and enjoying my own company so the timing was perfect. Had it been twelve months earlier, I probably would have never even considered it.

Since then I had built up my self-esteem and had more confidence and better ways of coping when things didn't go as I expected. My mindfulness training had helped with that and keeping calm and the work with Al-Anon helped me to know things would work out and I could give up my concerns to my guardian angel that I relied upon for support. It was my way of giving up control of everything and so far, it had been working for me. I wasn't scared and that shocked me, but I went with it.

Before, whenever I had thought about going away, I always came up with what I felt were valid reasons why I couldn't go. I had a flat, a mortgage. Where would I put all my things? I didn't want someone in my flat whilst I was away. How would I pay for everything? And so on.

You can talk yourself out of anything. If you tell yourself, you can't do something then your sub-conscious will immediately agree with you. That's right, you can't. I knew this was something I wanted to do and something I had to do for me, I knew I would feel so proud of myself once I had accomplished it. I was so excited and apprehensive at the same time.

I'd always dreamed of being a strong enough person to be able to go away by myself and feel content and happy with my own company. Now, the day had finally come.

The next six months was spent meticulously planning my trip. This was my way of feeling safe and in control. Of course, I was nervous and scared of the unknown – but having plans in place helped.

After speaking to people, I got some great tips about websites to look at, whether I needed a visa, places to visit and more. I found it enormously rewarding and loved researching the places I was going to visit. I did research on areas of America where I hadn't previously been; found areas that had events, scenery and attractions that I wanted to visit; and then decided on my route.

My trip would start in New York. I'd been before but only for a day or two so not long enough to have a good look around. After New York, I was off to Charleston in South Carolina, then Atlanta, New Orleans, Houston, Austin and Dallas and then to Memphis, Nashville and St. Louis. Finally, I would fly home from Chicago.

The months passed and the trip itinerary had many changes and updates. I learnt about Airbnb and discovered some reasonably priced places to stay. When you are single a lot of hotels charge a premium so the Airbnb route worked out well. I was nervous about staying in hostels but decided that I would try some just to see how it felt; I went for a branded group wherever I could because I thought it would be consistent in terms of cleanliness etc.

I built relationships with the people that I would be staying with, as it made me feel more safe and comfortable than with staying in a stranger's home. If I had to do it all again, I would be more than happy to just book my flights at the first place and then take it as it comes as it means I would have more flexibility.

It was hard to keep all my planning secret from my work colleagues. I wanted to tell them my plans but I was scared to lose my job before I left; so, I kept it all in which was hard to do. I started to grow my hair so that I had a less high-maintenance haircut; I collected boxes so I could store all my things in my flat; I contacted agencies to find someone to rent my flat; sorted out travel insurance and the money I needed. It was a busy time.

When I said, I wouldn't be extending my contract at work and the reasons why my manager was so excited for me. This was encouraging but took me by surprise as I wasn't expecting that reaction. I thought she wouldn't have cared or pleased that I was leaving. We did get on but we are very different personalities and I just felt I irritated her.

The agent I contacted managed to get me a tenant straight away which was great. So I moved out at the end of January and stayed at my Mum's for a month to save more money. I was also fortunate enough to have inherited some money from an old lady for whom I did a cleaning job and this enabled me to have some cash to fund part of the trip. It started costing me a lot more than I'd realised when I first had the idea of going travelling. I had a figure in my mind but it wasn't until I did the research I realised my estimate wasn't accurate.

Just before I was due to leave I'd arranged a night out with friends and family to say my goodbyes. Everyone wrote in a little book unbeknown to me which contained lovely messages and supportive comments. It was metallic purple on the outside, with a black swirly pattern overlaying it. It was only a small book (A6) and was full of useful tips and funny messages. It was nice that everyone came and we had a nice evening.

Mum, Simon (my Mum's partner), Daisy and I headed up to London Gatwick for my last day in the UK for three months. It was so odd - part of me was exceptionally nervous and the other part of me was feeling excited because I loved America and couldn't wait to see all the things I had researched.

Thankfully my nephews didn't come to the airport because I think I would have been a lot worse as I knew I would miss them terribly but we had Skype so I knew we would be speaking to each other.

On arrival, I got myself checked in and we all walked up to the restaurant area to grab some breakfast before my flight. I bought myself a selfie stick so got a few pictures of us all so that I had something with me. It was strange because I wanted to be with my family but at the same time I was excited and eager to start my journey in America.

When the time came to say our goodbyes, we were all in tears. I didn't want to leave my family and the familiarity that brought. But knew I needed to otherwise I never would. We gave each other the biggest of hugs and I headed through security for the start of my journey.

Chapter 31 – New York, Charleston and Atlanta

The flight to New York was amazing. I met a woman on the flight. When I sat down she was on the phone to her friend and she was deep in conversation, not long into the call I noticed she was crying; so, I handed her a tissue and after she got off the phone we started chatting.

We both introduced ourselves and she apologised for her upset which of course wasn't necessary, clearly something was on her mind. She explained it was about her boyfriend who I could relate to from my experiences in relationships, but she seemed in good spirits generally and moved the topic on quickly.

The plane was getting ready to leave and the hostesses were doing the usual checks, we both apprehensively decided to move seats as there were plenty to choose from. I always feel nervous about breaking rules and doing things I don't think I should, obviously, they usually sell the extra legroom seats for more so I knew we weren't meant to do it. Daisy wouldn't have cared; she is a born rule breaker. We opted for the extra legroom ones (who wouldn't!) and made ourselves comfortable for the 7 or so hour flight. We spent the next few hours talking which set my mind at ease about this massive decision I'd made to travel alone around America for the next three months.

It was great to have someone to talk to and the flight did go a lot quicker. We swapped numbers and said we'd keep in touch whilst she was in New York.

After my arrival at JFK I contacted my first host to let her know I was on my way. It was thick with snow, so when I arrived at my first home I had to drag my case through the snow and up a flight of stairs. I was feeling quite anxious because I wasn't sure where I was going - I stood at the door for a while before anyone answered. It was dark outside too so seeing the house numbers wasn't that easy.

Finally, I got in and met my host who was friendly. My room was adequate for what I needed; there were some other people in the house. I hadn't realised that so did feel a little uncomfortable but

It was all fine. I was worrying about nothing, but this was all new to me so I allowed myself to feel that way. I had a great night's sleep and woke up the next day ready to explore New York and all it had to offer.

The trip was a three-month personal development and self-discovery adventure. There were going to be ups and downs but I hoped to learn more about myself during the time I was away - it is always good to reflect on your experiences to see how far you have come.

New York was enjoyable. Five days wasn't long enough, not if you wanted to discover the neighbourhoods and see what they all had to offer. I stayed in Brooklyn but I visited a few different neighbourhoods by just hopping on and off the subway and taking a walk around.

Visiting Ground Zero was an experience which had me in tears. It was very touching to witness and the space was breath-taking. It was square in shape with a massive hole which housed a water feature, the water just falling into the pit beneath. Around the edge were the names and details of those that had lost their lives that day. People had left roses and flowers poking out of the holes where their names were etched out. To say it was moving is an understatement.

There was so much to see and do so whilst I was there I did a lot of the usual sightseeing attractions and bus tours and I went to the theatre to see 'Matilda', which was great, it reminded me of the book which I read as a child.

The lady I met on the flight got in touch and we did meet up when we both did the 'Sex in the City' bus tour which was good. The bus with its tour rep took a coach load of 'Sex in the City' fans around the key points in the city where filming took place for this well-known TV series. I must say I didn't remember a lot of the places but thankfully they showed a video on the coach to remind you of the scenes, unfortunately they showed it to us all after we visited the spot rather than before. I really enjoyed a stop off in a bar where the cast shared a cocktail.

After New York, I flew to Charleston in South Carolina. I knew little about it but it was on route so I thought why not stop there on the way. I picked up the car from the airport and I struggled to find my hosts house, it wasn't until after I got off the phone to her that I realised I had the sat nav set to walking mode instead of car mode. What an idiot! I was getting myself so stressed over nothing, it was trying to take me down no entry roads and pedestrian walkways.

Getting to my new home for the next week was a relief to say the least, it was a lovely bungalow house with a nice front garden and one of the American style post boxes which I thought were cool. I parked up and walked up to the front door, there were some lovely pottery painted ducks in the entrance. The door was open and I called out to my host. She came to the door and was friendly and welcoming.

She showed me my room and around the house which was a nice space. I had a walk-in wardrobe and a nice en-suite bathroom too. She had a daughter who she introduced me to, she seemed very chatty and whilst I was there she would tell me about her day at school and how many books she'd read.

Whilst I was in Charleston I got into a routine and visited the local swimming pool regularly. I quickly came to realise that there were not many public swimming pools in America; the only ones available were outside and not open until the summer. This was difficult because I was used to swimming three times a week. The routine of swimming was something I needed to help keep myself grounded.

Self Help Tips:

- Deep breathing is a great way to keep grounded and helps to be present in the moment, upper chest breathing causes anxiety so breath so you feel your ribs expand
- Having your feet firmly on the ground and imagining you are a tree is also a great grounding technique, imagining roots coming from your feet going deep underground
- Being in nature is grounding, a nice walk in a park or forest is good for the soul and can clear the head

My host and I often spent time together in the house chatting about life, men, work and our aspirations. It was great to be with someone on the same wavelength who was also into self-help and I really valued her time. I wasn't sure what to expect as I knew people had their own lives to get on with so it was a nice surprise to be able to connect with someone.

We had a lot of similar interests and she showed me her workshop area in the garage where she made pottery ducks and garden animals, just like the ones I saw on her porch. She ran classes locally for people living in homes and kids in school and they were popular.

The week seemed to fly by and after my time in Charleston I had to say my goodbyes and head to the airport for my next stop, Atlanta.

The check in and flight were fine and didn't take too long, on arrival in Atlanta my host met me at the airport in her convertible Mini and whisked me off for some dinner in a noodle bar which I thought was welcoming. She was very friendly and we got on really well, she is a business woman and helps people understand more about food allergies in the events industry.

We reached her house after dinner and she showed me around and my room. I got myself settled in and she was kind enough to take me to the local supermarket the next day so I could pick up some food to cook and for my lunches. One of the evenings my host took me to a place that she worked at, it was a cookery shop but also had a space for live food demonstrations.

My host was kind enough to get me a space so I could sit and participate with the other people that were attending. There were tables laid out and the chef and kitchen were at one end and we could all see what he was creating. It was something different and really interesting. They gave us the recipes for the food he was making, the pea hummus looked and tasted lovely and it was served with a nice crisp cracker which he made. I did feel a little awkward as I didn't know anyone of course, but I did get chatting to the people near me and shared my plans for my trip which was nice. There is a lot to be said for having someone to share your travel plans with. The evening went on for a good few hours and I had to wait for my host to finish work as she was helping the chef with all the preparations and serving up the food in the kitchen.

Once I had a day or so in Atlanta I took a walk around the local area and found a small park at the end of the road, there was a swing park with gym equipment outside which I had a go on and then a baseball area and bleachers (for those unaware that is the rows of seating next to the pitch). I had no clue what was going on but it was nice to sit and watch them, the weather was good and warm. The area near the park seemed quite run down and a local shop I passed had bars all around the window area which didn't make me feel safe.

The subway entrance wasn't far from the house and so I walked there and back every day to get into the centre of the city. The walk from the house to the subway took about 15 minutes; the sidewalks were quite uneven so I had to be careful where I was walking. Also there were quite big holes and dips in the road, I was surprised at the lack of maintenance in the area and my host told me that American's prefer not to pay taxes and accept things like this instead.

It made me think about home and how people wouldn't put up with that but then we pay a lot in taxes so I started to realise where our money was probably going. My hosts neighbour seemed nice and his name was Ed. My host introduced us and on one of the days we went to the park together and he explained about the softball game that was taking place.

It was so interesting talking to him, he was telling me about slavery in America and how racism is still such a big problem there. I just couldn't believe what I was hearing, I never really listen too much to the news and so I had no idea. I always had the perception that America was much more advanced than the UK but that wasn't the case. Ed wasn't married and he lived on his own, a very gentle and kind person who I was grateful to have met.

Chapter 32 – Atlanta and New Orleans (Yeah Baby)

My plan was to stay in Atlanta for two weeks but I quickly realised that this was too long - there wasn't a great deal to see and explore apart from Coca Cola World, which was amazing, I never knew so many of its drinks existed. When I went on the tour I did feel quite lonely because I couldn't seem to get chatting to people, they were either with partners or their families and when I did talk to people or try they looked at me strangely. So I kept myself to myself and walked around the tour to see how the drinks are made. The best bit was the room at the end which was full of all their drinks.

If you imagine walking into a room and there were about 10 different pod areas, on each area were lots of Coca Cola drink dispensers like you would see in a bar with the various drinks on them. Above each pod was a country and the drinks on the pod matched the country/area.

One of the main reasons I decided to visit Atlanta was because 'The Vampire Diaries' a TV series that I love, is partly filmed in Covington, not far away from Atlanta. I wanted to do one of their film tours and they had one for 'The Vampire Diaries' and the TV show 'Originals' which I also watched.

So, I hired a car for the day and drove out there. I did get a bit lost coming out of the airport where I hired the car from but once I was on the freeway it was OK. I have to say that I found it quite intimidating because the Americans have huge trucks and some of them were up behind me and I felt like an ant against them. It was quite tricky being on the other side of the car and the other side of the road but I did get used to it. I think it really built my confidence because I didn't really have a choice if I wanted to do things, which I did. If I wanted to go on the tour I needed a car because it wouldn't have been easy to get to otherwise.

Once I arrived in Covington I parked up and walked towards the office. The 'Mystic Falls' sign was outside the office which is where the TV series is set in the programme. The tour was a driving tour so you followed the main car. There was room left in the main car so as I was on my own they said I could join them instead of driving myself around. I was relieved because I felt nervous about following everyone, worrying I would get lost or that there wouldn't be space for me to park, or anything else my overthinking brain wanted to consider. The tour was amazing; it really brought to life the TV series I'd got addicted to. I took lots of photos and really enjoyed seeing where the filming took place and hearing inside information and details about what goes on with the cast. They had a shop full of memorabilia and life size cardboard cut outs of the actors. They also had a large map where you could place a pin from where you came from, so I put a pin in the south of England as close to home as I could.

The tour lasted all morning and I had some time afterwards to enjoy some lunch with three others I had chatted to during the tour. It's interesting finding out where others are from and what they are doing on their travels, how long they are travelling for or if they live in the area. I think it gives you so much culture and understanding of different people and their lives. After lunch it was time to go as I was booked onto another tour in the afternoon for 'The Originals'.

'The Originals' tour was in a different area so I had to drive myself there in time for the start. I did get a little lost and couldn't quite find where I was going but thankfully after calling the company they directed me in. I got to the reception and booked myself in and we waited for the tour rep to turn up. This was a walking tour so we just followed the tour guide to the various areas, I personally didn't think it was as good as the Vampire Diaries one but it was a newer show - it was interesting to understand more about the filming and how it portrays New Orleans although it was filmed on sets and in Covington.

They showed us areas which appear in the TV series and how it looks on screen and actually that certain archways or alleyways you thought were real, were actually foam or something similar. They explained how some of the shots taken make it look like it is in New Orleans but it isn't at all. I really loved being able to see things from a different perspective, I felt a lot more understanding of the film industry after hearing the various tricks used. The tour only lasted a few hours so afterwards I headed back to my car and started my journey back to the airport as I had to drop off the car.

Atlanta was difficult for me because I was there for so long. I started to feel quite alone. The days and nights were long and if my host was out or busy I didn't have people to talk to. You see when you walk down the street there isn't an atmosphere because a lot of people are in their cars, it is a bit like a ghost town. At home if you walk down the road you are likely to see people or you aren't far from them if you find a main street, so I found that quite difficult to get used to.

Having the ability to Skype family at home regularly helped to keep me going. I could share what was going on. It was hard being on my own, no matter how much I liked my own company. I did find it difficult to stay upbeat. I didn't want to walk the streets, visit attractions by myself and have no one to talk to. I soon realised the reason people book into hostels, so they are with other like-minded people.

My fear of hostels was founded on sharing with a group of unknown women and being kept awake or not feeling safe, which is why I opted for the Airbnb. I suppose they both come with positives and negatives and it's just a matter of trying things to see how you feel.

When the time came, I was ready to leave Atlanta and excited about my next stop which was New Orleans. I love jazz and music and I'd heard great things from my friend so couldn't wait to explore. I said my goodbyes to Ed and my host and headed to the airport for my flight to New Orleans.

Once I arrived in New Orleans I made my way to my host's house by taxi. I decided to save money on things like food and cook for myself so I could save the money for taxis getting from the airport to where I was staying.

I think everyone prioritises their money and some saved it for alcohol, making sure I could easily get somewhere safely was my priority.

When I arrived, no one was home and I couldn't get hold of my host. I started to panic and I wasn't feeling comfortable. My fears started creeping in, my head started to over-worry but eventually my host contacted me and told me where to find the key so I could let myself in.

I was staying in an area outside of the main New Orleans centre. It took about 20 minutes to get there on the bus. I managed to find my way around and where the bus stops were. It was so hot in New Orleans so standing around wasn't ideal but buses weren't always as regular as the ones at home.

I stayed in New Orleans for around 10 days and it was the best time. I just immersed myself in music and movies; I learnt it's the cheapest place for film companies to use to produce films, so there were a lot of movie trucks parked up on the streets. On one movie tour I went on, we were told that Brad Pitt and Al Pacino were filming that week, how exciting! We did drive by Brad Pitt's home and Sandra Bullock's home too. I was totally star struck; I love the movies and the glamour of it all but in reality I know it isn't quite like that. There is a lot of standing around and waiting for the cast and extras.

On the movie tour, I met a group from Alabama and they were so kind to me. They said I could come along with them to lunch which I did and we enjoyed some amazing dishes. One of my favourites was gumbo which can be described as a type of stew served with rice, it was delicious. Another dish was Jambalaya; this was a spicier dish with meat or fish or both, very delicious. It was good to be with other people and have some company. I still felt a little awkward because I was the only one that didn't know everyone; but they were friendly.

After our lunch, we said our goodbyes and went our separate ways. I stayed to listen to the live music in the streets; people would just sit or stand around the street and watch the music, chipping some money into pots they'd left out. One lady went into a shop and bought a pack of beer for one group which was a nice touch, they got a great round of applause when she set it down on the street where they were playing.

Venturing into bars on my own was another big step for me. I felt proud of myself that I was pushing myself to do things out of my comfort zone, but at the same time felt sorry for myself, and upset that I was having to do it all alone. I made the choice to travel alone of course; and I accept that, I just wanted to meet others I could be with more of the time.

Whilst I was in New Orleans the Easter parade was on which was so much fun. People threw beaded necklaces to the crowd and I had so many my neck was hurting from the weight of them! It was a great atmosphere, with people who were having fun dancing, singing and even the passing cars getting involved. Unfortunately, I missed Mardi Gras but not by much but I heard it was an amazing experience, maybe next time.

I did meet someone in a bar one day. I'd been on a swamp

tour in the morning and then got dropped off in the main New Orleans streets by one of the guys I met on the tour. I wandered around and came across a bar which felt inviting so I thought why not so I went inside and ordered myself a drink.

The bar was in the centre with bar stools set around it, I sat between two guys and ordered a Bacardi and coke. It didn't take long to realise that the measures in America compared to England were double the amount or close to it, they don't really use measures. I started chatting to the guys and sort of flipped between them for a while as one was friendlier than the other. I did feel nervous and a bit stupid at times, part of me felt I was trying too hard and to relax and just sit and enjoy my drink. I did think that if I sit and enjoy my drink and they are interested in chatting they will. I ended up chatting to the guy on my left in the end who was the quieter of the two and chatted about our day. He was there on a business event for a few days.

After a while he asked if I had any plans for the rest of the evening which I didn't so we agreed to go to another bar and grab some dinner. It did feel weird because I was in a foreign country with a guy I didn't really know, but he seemed nice and I trusted my gut instinct. We walked down the road hand in hand and stopped every now and then to kiss each other. It was a real buzz for me because I hadn't had any affection like this for a long time, I was so happy.

We found somewhere to eat and the lady in the restaurant assumed we were a couple which was a little awkward. We seemed to have a lot to chat about, although there were moments of silence and I felt a little awkward. I think I was getting irritable about where the evening was going. I was still struggling with going with the flow, just enjoying the moment for what it was. We went for another drink after the meal and sat at the bar, chatting to the barman. There wasn't much of an atmosphere and there was boxing on the TV and people were sat having a meal behind us. I felt more and more frustrated and I think he could tell something was up. It did annoy me that I was getting myself in a state but I did my best to keep my annoyance under wraps.

We left the bar and just started walking, I wasn't really sure where we were going but we ended up at his hotel. Finally I knew where the night was going and he took me by the hand inside the hotel. We made our way into the lift up to his room.

I had a wonderful time and it was great to be in a man's company again, he was a real gentleman. It was exciting and a bit risky but that was part of the fun of it. He called me a cab and I headed back to my host's house.

My host was in and out most of the time I was at the house, she was a head teacher at a local school and she had a little Chihuahua dog which I think she kept locked in her room every day, whilst I wasn't a big dog fan I wasn't sure that was a good idea.

When we were both in the house we would chat about the differences of America and the UK, I found it really fascinating. We talked about racism, taxes, presidents and everything in between. The more and more I spoke to Americans the more I realised how behind they were compared to the UK.

It's very insightful when you speak to people in different cultures and understand that actually we have very similar issues no matter where we live. After ten days in New Orleans it was time to move onto my next destination which was Houston.

My favourite pastime in New Orleans

The famous New Orleans Beignets

Chapter 33 – Houston and Austin

Houston was a completely different experience. It was my first hostel and I arrived at a beautiful place on a leafy street. The house was stunning and not the typical hostel I had imagined. It looked like a historic building and was surrounded by a lovely bright green lawn at the front with a pathway from the pavement right down the middle leading up to a bright red front door. I opened the heavy door and walked into the reception area, I checked in and familiarised myself with the shared areas. I sat outside in the heat which was lovely and had a call with my sister Daisy to let her know I got there safely and everything was OK.

Once the dormitory was ready they showed me to my bed. There were eight beds in total and an en-suite bathroom. It was clean enough and everyone had a locker to put their valuables in and we just put our suitcases wherever there was a space. The hostel had a swimming pool so I was happy (although it wasn't clean looking).

I settled in and got chatting to three guys on my first night. It was good to be with other travellers - they were from France, Canada and Poland. We chatted long into the night about our travels, where we had been and where we were going next. The man from Poland was only away for a few weeks and was packing in a lot in that time. I came to realise that a lot of travellers only stayed in one place for a few days; not longer to see the whole city, which is what I wanted to do. I wanted to get a feel of how the locals lived - what they do on their time off and so on. Having at least a week in each place allowed me to do that.

The first day I was in Houston we decided to go to Houston Space Centre. This is where I discovered Google Maps; I had heard of it but not used it that much. I was getting around by using my satnav, but it didn't give me the details of where I needed to get a bus, and what number, and what stop I should get off.

Google Maps was a life saver for me once I knew about how it worked. I felt so much more comfortable knowing I didn't need to worry about the transport side of things which is a challenge in America because the public transport isn't that great in places.

I visited a great carnival whilst I was in Houston - all the cars were 'dressed' up in all sorts of ways, and there were bikes and people on stilts. There were hundreds of them and it seemed to go on forever. It was great fun and so colourful. I walked down the street and took in the atmosphere, watching the kids playing with their balloons, eating corndogs and having fun. Seeing people with corndogs made me want to try it, so I went up to one of the food trailers and bought my own. It's a frankfurter sausage on a stick covered in a type of batter and deep fried. I enjoyed it, I love frankfurters anyway but the outside covering the sausage made it easy to eat but I need ketchup so I had to try and balance it on a vertical hotdog in effect, which was quite tricky.

Myself and a girl I met at the hostel decided to go to a

basketball game; although it was unbelievably expensive we thought it was a once in a lifetime thing. We paid for our tickets after much debate and entered the rather intimidating sized stadium. I have never experienced anything like it, there were bars and places to get food as usual but it was so big. Lots of people of course and you could take alcohol inside the basketball seating area.

We were sat quite far back but could see clearly enough, it was strange because people seemed to come and go, it wasn't like a football match at home I'd been to. People come in and sit and stay until half time, have a break and then come back. The stadium never really looked full. They did a lot of entertainment in between the breaks which was quite fun to watch, one of them was a couple who would bring their child onto the basketball court and they had laid out a mat which was split into lanes. The child had to crawl from one parent to the other and whichever one got to the end the quickest was the winner, it was hilarious.

Sadly, the next day I was about to go to a place called Galveston with a guy at the hostel as it had been recommended and I went to find my camera to take with me and realised I didn't have it, I looked everywhere and it wasn't to be found. It was gone and I lost over six weeks' worth of pictures. It was such a shame because it wasn't something I could get back, but what's importance is that I still have the memories of my experiences. It can be easy to get attached to possessions but really no one can take away what you have been through, it's always there.

Unfortunately my luck in losing things was to continue. When I went to Galveston (beautiful place by the sea), I lost my wallet. It wasn't until I went to pay for something I realised it was missing. My heart sank - my cards, ID and everything was in there. Thankfully I did have some cash back at the hostel, and another card, but it was a massive inconvenience. I couldn't recall where I might have lost it and we travelled back and retraced our steps, I didn't feel it had been stolen because we hadn't been anywhere for it to get taken or near other people.

I was proud of myself, as I managed to stay calm through the whole saga. Others were saying they would have been in a mess about it. I just accepted what had happened and got on with organising replacements cards, a practical approach. My friend that I went with was really kind and lent me his phone so I could call my banks and try and sort out replacement cards and contact my Mum to explain that I'd need her to post them out to me.

Insider Tip:

Those affected by someone's drinking are excellent in a crisis because that's what they are used to living with, however they find more day to day encounters more difficult to deal with.

Luckily for me someone found it and handed it into a police station. He said he found it in the middle of the road and when he described it I recall where it was, I was hunting in my bag for something at the time. You know when you just can't find what you are looking for then suddenly the item is right there in front of you. My wallet must have fallen out in my search. By the time I arrived at my next destination in Dallas I had it back in my possession but not before it had its own little detour due to it being addressed wrong. Although the cards had been cancelled I did have my money back. What a massive relief and what a lovely gesture of a stranger to take the time to send it back to me.

After Houston, I moved onto Austin and another hostel. It was the same group as the previous one and in a really beautiful location right by the water's edge. On my arrival I explained I was waiting for my cards so they knew to expect them. They showed me to my room and explained about breakfast and where I could leave any food I bought. The first day I was there I walked up to the local supermarket which was about a 30 minute walk and with heavy bags of food it was only something I did once.

In the mornings there were cereals, fruit and bread to help yourself to. Typical American breakfasts seemed to consist of peanut butter, jam and Nutella. They weren't exactly pro on healthy eating but that was ok because I tended to buy my own food and cook for myself. Some local companies donated bread and pastries which was a treat, I thought it was really kind of them to think of people like us that were on a limited budget.

There were several English people staying in this hostel so I got to talk to people from home for the first time in about six weeks which was great. There were other Americans that seemed to be travelling either for work or they wanted to move to the area. Others were travelling around on a trip like me.

During my stay, I visited some amazing places. Colin (one of the guys in the hostel) had a truck, so he could take us to places we would have never been able to get to. Julie, Moe, Colin and I hung around together whilst we stayed in Austin, Moe was from Germany, Julie from France and Colin from Australia. They were great people and Moe was hilarious, with such a dead pan sense of humour – and German which is rare!

On one of the days Colin, Moe and myself decided to head off to Hamilton Pool, it was somewhere I had investigated before I left for my trip and it didn't disappoint. It was intensely beautiful with a steep walk down to it but once you got there it was worth it. None of the others had heard of it or knew it existed so I think they were grateful that we made the effort to drive there, as it wasn't close to the hostel.

We all enjoyed a swim and relaxed for an hour or so, the place limited the number of people that could enter at any one time. I swam to where one of the waterfalls were and just swimming underneath it and feeling so grateful of the experience. I kept thinking I'm finally here; the place I saw on the internet is now a reality. We didn't stay that long before we decided to check out some of the surrounding area, it was so beautiful, we didn't get there until later in the day so we had to keep our walk short as they were due to close for the day.

In the evenings we would chill out and play some games, I stayed and chatted to whoever was about which was nice because you could have company when you wanted it and not when you didn't.

In the hostel Colin was the driver and he worked in the

Australian army and one of the days he asked if we wanted to go to a gun range. Moe, Julie and I joined him. Firing a gun was an interesting experience, and I didn't do too badly but I felt apprehensive each time because of the kick-back. Having something so powerful at my fingertips made me feel safe but at the same time as I was new to it, completely nervous.

We did have a discussion between us about having guns and how we felt about it, a lot of people in America have them and use them for hunting etc. and obviously, a lot don't. I think you need to know what you are doing with a gun as they aren't a toy. With something so powerful comes responsibility and knowing you aren't going to use it whenever your ego kicks in is the difference between life and death at times, or certainly serious injury.

One of the evenings a group of us went to watch the bats that live underneath the Ann W. Richards Congress Avenue Bridge. There were a lot of people there and they were all waiting for the bats to come out at night which they did from March to November. I think I was expecting it to be a big black mass of bats but it wasn't, they all came out at different times. It was still a sight to see.

In the day I would lay out in the hammock in the garden to catch some rays, the weather was beautiful. Other times I took myself out on the kayaks which were at the lake just in front of the hostel. I felt so relaxed, I loved being out on the water and just kayaked around the area, watching the local wildlife, small turtles were resting on the thinnest of branches and when they heard me approaching they just popped off into the water. It was so peaceful and so breath-taking,

I loved the simplicity of it and freedom to go and do what I fancied.

I stayed in Austin for about eleven days which was the right length of time for me. I didn't feel it was as musical as people said, it could be because I went to different areas or not at the right times. There were bars and music of course but the vibe wasn't the same as New Orleans. New Orleans was much buzzier when it came to the music and I think it was because a lot of it was out in the street, it was a real raw way of seeing music, people using bits of plastic and buckets and such like to make sounds.

My first hostel in Houston

My new friends at the Houston Hostel

At the car show in Houston

My first Corn Dog

**My friends at Austin Hostel
(Moe far left and Colin next to him)**

Ready for the Bats to make their appearance

View from the Hostel in Austin
To the far left is the Kayaking hire

Amazing artwork in Austin

Me and My target

The beautiful Hamilton Pool

Chapter 34 – Dallas, Memphis, Nashville, St Louis and Chicago

After my time in Austin I made my way to Dallas on the coach this time. It was slow due to the traffic but it was a nice change from flights. I was lucky enough to be staying with a work colleague's friends. They didn't live in Dallas itself but a smaller place called Grapevine - of all the places this was one of my favourites. Chris picked me up from the coach station and we introduced ourselves and got to know a bit more about each other and how he knew my work colleague.

Chris and his wife had a beautiful home, swimming pool and they loaned me their car for the week! I had a lovely spacious room with an en-suite and felt extremely welcomed and comfortable immediately. The next day I went out and visited the local town which was so beautiful; tasted the local cuisine (brisket is popular there) and wandered around some of the quaint shops.

One of the days I took myself off to a place called Fort Worth, where they had a rodeo, and a stockyard. They did tours which I booked myself onto, they took us around what were the old stockyards, where the animals were kept and the history. As we walked around they pointed out an area that was used for the filming of a TV series called Prison Break which I watched in my five weeks off work when I had my operation.

Walking around the town taking it all in was great fun, the atmosphere was very inviting and on the tour they pointed out the Stockyards hotel where Bonnie and Clyde were arrested. I went into a local Honkey Tonk which was a bar, it was huge with lots of pool tables, dance floors and bars. I wanted to go back in the evening because I thought it would be really buzzy and to see some real American country dancing would have been fun, but I wasn't really interested in doing it on my own.

Texas was all about country and I really wanted to experience a rodeo, so one evening Chris, his wife and I went to see what it was like. We drove back to Fort Worth where I had been previously, I absolutely loved the rodeo and realised I do like country music and the whole country scene. It was a completely different environment to what I'm used to but I felt right at home. When we came out of the rodeo there was live music outside and people were dancing and it looked such fun, I wanted to stay but Chris's wife wasn't feeling well so we headed home for the evening. I was disappointed by I couldn't really stay because I had no way of getting back to the house.

One of the days I visited the local mint where all the money was made which I found fascinating, you walk around with a headset and listen to all the different tasks that go on and the security involved. You walk in a walkway which is elevated over the factory area so you can see people at work. I loved it and found the details of how the templates for the dollars are made very insightful. Later in the day I spent some time just relaxing by the pool and did a call home to the family to see how everyone was.

I did keep in touch with everyone regularly and I was also writing a blog each day about my experience so I had something to look back on.

Later that evening my host Chris took me out on his motorbike for a ride. It was a mix between nervous and exhilarating in an apprehensive way. Let's just say it didn't convert me into an avid fan. I felt far too vulnerable on the back.

Some of the days I would go out first thing and explore and then come back later in the afternoon and chill by the pool. Dallas was probably the most confusing place I drove in my entire trip. I found the road signs very confusing, they seemed to appear in the wrong place in my mind and I often had to go back on myself to get where I needed to be. The traffic was really bad too. When I was back at the house it was great to finally be able to swim whenever I wanted to. They had this amazing pool cleaner, it was called a 'Kreepy Krauly' so if you Google it you'll see what it looks like. I was fascinated with it, I thought it was such a clever device and with my love of technology it really entertained me. It would go around the pool by itself and suck up the twigs, leaves and anything it could out of the pool so it was nice and clean.

When I was laying in the sun Chris and Lizann's dog would come and lay in the sun and alternate between that and the shade when it got too hot. Dallas was beautiful in terms of the weather and I was on a mission to get a tan as it was a standing joke with Daisy in the past I would come back from holiday still white.

As the days, weeks and months went on I felt proud of my

achievements. I often give myself a hard time about not being, doing and having enough but sometimes I have to remember to celebrate my successes and feel proud. It makes me feel exceptionally grateful.

Insider Tip:

Expectations and being overly responsible is common in those living with an alcoholic. They have a lot to be responsible for as the drinker is absent both physically and mentally so everyone else must chip in.

I've kept in touch with my hosts from each destination and would go back to Dallas, as well as New Orleans. I enjoyed both places very much.

After Dallas, I arrived at Memphis - probably one of the most traumatic times of my trip. When I arrived at the airport in Dallas I was asked my weight and height. I was surprised when they told me it was a nine-seater plane! Panic set in.

The plane absolutely terrified me. There were only three passengers plus the pilot and co-pilot. After taking off we had to stop in other places to pick up more people. It was awful. The feeling of the plane suddenly dropping and moving from side to side sent me over the edge and I thought I was going to die. I was so scared and just wanted to get off.

Once we finally landed in Memphis, I picked up my car and drove to the hostel. I parked up and went to the only door I could find with a bell, I was all set to check in, only to find that no one was answering the phone or available to open the door.

I wasn't in the best state after my flight so I went to a local bar and ordered some dinner and just sat and felt sorry for myself.

This was the last straw in a stressful day; I just sat there in tears and had to go off to the toilet to get myself together. I was constantly trying to get through to the hostel by phone and no one was answering so after a long time I gave up. I decided to find a hotel to stay in for the night and face the hostel the next day.

The hostel eventually called me but I explained about the effects of the terrible flight and how having no access to the hostel just made things worse. I said I would come back the following day as I just didn't feel safe or comfortable or have the energy to sort it out that night. They understood and the guy apologised profusely but I didn't want to hear it.

The hotel I stayed at was in another part of town and was fine for one night. I felt a big sigh of relief once I got there and settled into my room. I got a good night sleep and in the morning had some breakfast and a swim in their pool and headed off to the hostel. On my arrival, they apologised and we had a brief chat about the previous day to clear the air. It was interesting as there was some learning for me in this event - I listened to myself and did what I thought I needed to do, rather than what someone else wanted. I knew that I wasn't in a good place; but that it would be fine the next day. Previously I think I would have thought it was worse than it was. Now I believe that whilst I still and probably always will have anxiety I recover from any attacks a lot quicker than before and I don't panic to the same degree either.

I stayed in Memphis for five days and met some lovely people. I visited Graceland which was a highlight of the trip - the house was just as Elvis had left it. It was interesting to see all his awards, outfits, cars and aeroplanes. Standing by his grave in the grounds was eerie, everyone had headsets on listening to the audio as you walked around. There were a lot of people there just being present and taking it all in.

Other than Graceland I didn't like Memphis as there was not a lot to do and I felt it wasn't looked after - people had told me this before I went there so that's why I didn't stay longer.

After Memphis, I had to fly to Nashville. This was going to be the same aeroplane as before so I was feeling anxious again. I got to the airport at around 6:30am only to discover my flight was cancelled and no one had informed me. They offered me another flight at 10:00am but I wasn't happy about it and looked at getting a coach. I found a Greyhound bus that went to Nashville so I booked that instead. A blessing in disguise as I didn't want to fly on that type of plane ever again!

On arrival at the Greyhound bus station with my ticket I queued up to get on. There were some discussions which I couldn't hear until I was told through someone else in the queue that the bus was full. This wasn't the best start to my day. Not only had my flight been cancelled but the bus was full. I had to wait until the afternoon to get the next bus.

I finally arrived in Nashville later than anticipated but my hosts were kind and understanding. In life, you just cope with what is thrown at you and get on with it - not something I was comfortable with but I adapted more and more as my trip when on.

My time in Nashville was short. I only stayed for around five days and whilst it was a pleasant place I wouldn't go back I just didn't feel there was a lot going on and without a car you couldn't explore much. My hosts were great - we chatted a lot and I went on a night out with the lady of the house. We had fun dancing in a local bar.

After Nashville I went to St. Louis which was OK but not one of my favourite destinations. The Gateway Arch was quite cool; you travelled in tiny pods up to the top - again this was out of my comfort zone but I did it! I did feel anxious inside as you couldn't sit up straight and I was on my own. My stomach was going around but I kept doing my breathing exercises and that helped to calm me down.

Something that I did overcome in St Louis was my fear of dogs. My hosts had three dogs and they would bark as I walked up to the front door. I thought I needed to reassure them – I'm ok and they are ok - so I would talk to them as I walked through the door and even reached out to stroke them. My stomach was in knots and I was scared, but I made myself do it because I thought I need to get over this.

Thankfully it got easier with time and since being back in the UK my relationship with dogs has changed - I enjoy them now as opposed to shying away from them.

My last stop was Chicago. By this point I was ready to come home, I was tired of being on my own; and realised being in hostels was the answer. Regular Skype calls and Facebook messages did help - people cheered me up and I knew I had to keep going. It is easy to just give in but then where would that get us?

The unknown can be scary but then everything is the first time we do it.

I didn't have the best arrival in Chicago. My host was not friendly and gave me a few rules when I got there - she didn't want me using the upstairs, even though that had been advertised, and she wasn't too happy that I would be cooking. My room was in the basement and quite dark - I had my own entrance; but I felt marginalised and that no one wanted to interact with me. The impression I got via email before I left the UK was different to the reality of the situation.

I did a lot of exploring in Chicago. I'd met up with a friend of my host in Atlanta; and she gave me some great tips. I enjoyed the Willis Tower and visiting the local attractions such as the famous Chicago Bean which is a huge silver mirrored bean shaped structure in Millennium Park.

By this time, I was running out of money, so I would hop on the subway and then get off at different stops and walk around the neighbourhoods and see what was happening. I also discovered Dunkin Donuts Iced Coffees which were amazing and I got completely addicted to them!

I did feel as if I was counting down the days until I left which made me sad as I would rather have not wanted to go home. If the place I had stayed in was better, it would have made a difference. I do love my independence but it made me realise how important the relationships of friends and family are to me and what a different it makes.

You can be anywhere in the world but if the important people aren't with you and people you want there to share the experience, for me it isn't as powerful.

The Americans are very friendly and it really shocked me throughout my trip the extent that they would go to for someone that they barely knew. For example, I met a great couple in a local taco place who were friendly; we got chatting in the restaurant at the bar and I was sharing my story and travel insights and they were filling me in on their stories. One of the guys was actually born in the UK and moved to the USA after being in the military, the other guy was an American and worked with research and looking at social and environmental issues.

We were probably in the taco bar for a good couple of hours and they suggested going to their place for some food. It was literally across the road from the taco bar, the place was lovely and on three floors. Just inside the door was a large lounge area then stairs up to the kitchen which overlooked the lounge beneath. They prepared the food and cocktails for the evening, we were having a barbeque which was going to be on the roof terrace, all very posh. Up another set of stairs to the bedrooms and bathroom and another lounge area which then led to the loft.

It was so pretty with plants all around the edge of the balcony, the barbeque all set up with the smell of food cooking away. It was funny because one of them was quite drunk and he was the chef so we were a little worried about how the food was going to turn out as he was cooking lobster. It was all delicious and I just sat there feeling very thankful that I'd met these guys and how hospitable they were to me.

252

We chatted into the evening about all sorts of topics but eventually it was time to leave so I said my goodbyes and we added each other to Facebook and I left to head home for the night as I had a long day ahead.

The morning of my departure I was feeling super excited! I left for the airport and got a bus to the subway station and then it took me straight to the airport. I checked in and made myself comfortable in the departure lounge, excited in anticipation. My flight home was not as good as on the way out, I couldn't really get comfortable and the guy next to me wasn't very chatty so it made it a long flight. On my arrival, back to the UK I arrived before my Mum and friend Hayley. I didn't want to come out of the departure lounge until they were there - the worst thing about coming back from a holiday is coming through arrivals to no one! It was great to see a friendly face and I gave my Mum and Hayley a big hug. It was lovely to be back in the UK and home again.

We arrived at Mum and Simon's house because I was going to be staying with them for a while as my flat was still rented out and I couldn't go back there straight away but that was OK as I was happy not to. It took some time to get myself settled back home again but it was not as bad as it could have been, I had somewhere to live and a car - I just needed to find a job and somewhere more permanent to live.

Mum and Simon put me up for a few months before I found somewhere new. It was interesting actually because I was apprehensive about living with my Mum again, thinking we would be arguing all the time and I would be constantly frustrated at her but it was OK. Of course we had moments but generally we got on and I had a great laugh with them. It didn't take too long to find a new job, I was enjoying having the time back to catch up with friends and family if I'm honest. I managed to get a temporary job with the NHS; and then got head-hunted for another role which I took as it was the same money but for part-time hours. This was important, because I wanted to get my business up and running.

If you want to know more about my discoveries and experiences in the United States you can read more on my blog which I kept up every day: http://myamericaexpedition.blogspot.co.uk. There is so much more to share but I just wanted to highlight some of the major challenges I faced during my trip.

Time to Reflect

Well, what can I say? This was the most transformational trip of my life. To think I even went alone still astounds me now, I have to pinch myself. I feel totally grateful for the opportunity and I feel proud that I pushed through my fears and did it anyway (thank you Susan Jeffers).

There were a number of highs and lows during the trip and I feel very proud of how I handled them. My intention isn't to sound big headed but for my whole life I have given myself a hard time about not being, doing or achieving enough.

The biggest issues that I faced of course were losing my wallet, camera and being away from my friends and family. To push through the low times and reassure myself was a big achievement for me, it's easy to turn to others to make ourselves feel better but when we can sooth ourselves it's much more nourishing. I haven't mastered this by any means but I'm like wine, improving with age.

The people I met, the stories I heard and the places I visited are gifts, memories I will have for the rest of my life. Even though I lost my camera those memories are in my brain and I hope I'll never forget them, certainly the important ones will remain I'm sure. I learnt about another culture and how other people live in America, understanding more about slavery and how racism is still an issue there was eye opening.

Making new friends and trusting in whatever happened was reassuring, my confidence built during those three months because each time I did something that I was a little uncomfortable I felt excitement and pride, that increased with every small achievement I overcame.

Something else I think I learnt was the ability to be more flexible and adaptable because not everything I prepared before I left went to plan, even things I arranged in America didn't happen as I hoped or wanted but I learnt to go with it and adapt. That has definitely impacted on my life now and I'm very grateful that I have shifted from the rigid life I once lived.

I want to say a very big thank you to everyone I met whilst I was away, it was a pleasure.

Chapter 35 – Home Sweet Home

Getting back to normality takes time but once I had a job and a new place to live it was a lot easier. I found a room in a lovely house fifteen minutes away from Bournemouth. It was just the landlady and her son living there and I had a lovely big room with en-suite bathroom. It did take time to find the right place but when I saw the room and the house I knew immediately that it was ideal, not far from my new job in Wimborne and not far from Bournemouth for all my business work.

It was great to get some normality back in my life, seeing friends, getting my business together (learning a lot on the way); and getting a routine established - going to work, and swimming again.

After getting back from America I got back in touch with my ex-fiancé Matt after my trip. I was chatting to his sister in law whilst I was travelling as they live in Oklahoma. It was nice to have someone at hand to chat to that knew me whilst I was away and she was a great support when I felt low. It was about fifteen years since I'd spoken to Matt but it was good to be in contact again. We met up a few times and kept in touch by text when I was home. He's great to talk to and business-minded so I could run things past him to get his views on my ideas.

Once I was back into the swing of things I started to support my local football team - AFC Bournemouth, and have become an avid fan. I haven't missed a match yet! Matt is also a supporter, so that was another interest we had to talk about. We would meet before the game for a drink and discuss the predicted score and how the team were doing. I'm not sure what made me want to get back in touch with him again but I'm glad I did because we are extremely similar.

After renting for a while I started to realise I had no permanence. I had none of my things around me and kept having to go back to the flat to pick bits up. I was tired of going back and forth to Bournemouth to meetings and it was starting to get difficult to meet up with people. I found I was hanging around in Bournemouth or staying overnight because it wasn't worth going home.

So, I decided I needed to move back into my flat, and gave notice to my tenants. I hadn't been that bothered before but as time went on I realised how much I missed being there and having all my things. I felt safe there; which is very important to me after living in such a volatile environment as a child.

Since coming back from America my confidence has grown. I feel I can achieve anything; I'm more relaxed about things; and I can cope better when things don't always go to plan. Just because a situation may be uncomfortable, it doesn't mean my whole life is a disaster. It just means things are rubbish in the moment, but they will get better.

After spending a lot of time developing my business, I realised there is a lot to it! I love to learn but the pressure I can place on myself can be immense. It's easy for me to compare to others and to feel bad that I'm not doing as well as them. I keep telling myself that I'm not them and I'm working at my pace in the way in which suits me not them.

Previously I did start a business, offering one-to-one therapy. For whatever reason, it didn't work, but now I feel that this is my time and this is going to happen. My intention is to be an inspirational and motivational speaker - I want to use my experience of living in an alcoholic home.

Businesses evolve over time, and you must have patience and perseverance. It would be easy to give up because you have no customers, but you can't, or where would you be? I love freedom and choice and having my own business gives me that.

I do believe in myself and know I can do it. I've overcome a massive amount since I was young and I can honestly say I'm proud of my achievements. They haven't come easily, and I've worked hard for them, although at the time I think I'm just doing what is needed, I realise that's because I have high expectations.

Having the right support around me to help me when I'm struggling is so important, not just in business but in life. Thankfully I've some great friends that are always around to listen. They can't always solve the problem but they are there for me and I'm exceptionally honoured to have them in my life.

Now I do the things that I enjoy and that make me happy - meditation is one, and singing is another. I enjoy music workshops - my friend runs one which is all to do with improvisation. You make a beat on a drum or shake a maraca and others join in and before you know it you have an amazing tune.

I love immersing myself with like-minded people, usually creative types, people who enjoy music, self-help, psychology and wellbeing. Swimming is something I consider to be a staple part of my being, I've never drifted in and out of it, I've done it since a child and so it seems effortless to me now, apart from having to get up at 6:30am, that doesn't always feel effortless.

Home cooking is another passion of mine and doing what I can to be as healthy as possible. I'd love to have a garden where I can grow all my own vegetables and then use that in my cooking. How fulfilling would that be?

It's important to think about what you like, and who you enjoy being around. Not until the last few years have I fully understood where my passions lie. I feel elated when I sing; and I feel connected with others when I'm meditating or talking about psychology or NLP.

The people I surround myself with are generally on the same wave length as me; which means my life is always full of the things I love, with the people that I enjoy being with. This is a long way from my childhood state, where everything I did was designed to please others or avoid being alone.

It's important for me to be open and try new things, just because it may not *feel* right doesn't mean it *isn't* right. Our comfort zone would be saying, "No this is scary!"; but we can push past that.

We need to take risks; and that is what I've been doing done these past few years.

So, I moved back to my flat. I swim at my local pool; I have more time at home, and I love having all my things around me. I continue to work on my business; and there have been highs and lows. Sometimes I feel I'm putting in a lot of effort and getting little in return. Sometimes I feel I try too hard; and must remember I need to let things flow, and create a balance between expecting things to come and taking steps to help things move along.

Getting a balance at times can be difficult; I'm so black and white in my outlook and shades of grey are not something I'm familiar with. This is a typical trait of a child of an alcoholic.

After returning from America I decided to find a new choir and I still have the odd singing lesson here and there. The choir I'm in now is a soul choir and we are aiming to get more gigs where we can, our teacher has high expectations and wants us to be really good. The tricky thing is everyone comes for different reasons, some practice and some don't. Some are musical and some aren't, I don't read music I tend to go with my ear and pitch a note based on what I hear. We all have different experience but as time goes on we are learning faster and remembering the arrangements and our confidence is building. After a few months, I was encouraged to do a solo at an event they were holding, just for the singers at the music school and I pushed myself to do it. Feel the fear and do it anyway!

My teacher was supportive and helped me to feel less anxious - I also discovered Bach remedies which are good for helping with anxiety. Breathing is also another great technique to use; it keeps you focussed and calms you.

On the night, I was still feeling quite apprehensive but I did it! I got my nephew to record me and it sounded fine. I could feel that my voice was affected by my nerves, I knew I had to hold the microphone in a certain way, move, remember the words and look like I was enjoying it. So not too much to think about really! I have sung another solo since, which went better, and I'm keeping up the performances so that I don't lose my confidence. If you stop doing it then you have to start all over again to build your confidence, but taking small steps is better than none at all.

Although I recently lost my part-time job - and still tend to feel worry and panic on occasions - deep down I know that things will work out. Since going to Al-Anon and learning to meditate, I've discovered that having faith and trusting in something takes the weight off my shoulders. I believe I've a guardian angel looking over me - she knows the big plan and I just leave it up to her. It gives me a sense of peace which is something I didn't have for a long time.

It's normal to have these feelings; now I give myself permission to feel this way and reassure myself that it is fine to not get things right all the time, not know everything or know what to do or what will happen. This has been a learning curve for me as is everything in life. We don't just learn in a classroom; we learn anywhere if we are paying attention.

Chapter 36 – Deja Vu

It's always been important to me to help others. Listening to people talk and offer help and advice, sometimes without being asked is what I do. My intentions were always good.

This hasn't changed now I'm 41; and after becoming more aware of what I care about, and what's important to me I felt I wanted to do more. I wanted to raise awareness and support those like me that have been affected by alcoholism. In part that is why I wrote this book; it is not just for children of alcoholics but for anyone that needs inspiration or motivation.

Looking at the disastrous home life, experiences and relationships I experienced I've turned it around and become a better person. I'm strong-willed, but life is about choices, we make them every day. It just depends on which ones you make, and which direction you go in. But remember that they are YOUR choices, no one else's, and dishing out blame when things go wrong never gets you anywhere but I accept we all still do that.

At times, it can be hard to realise that we don't always take responsibility for things that happen in our life. I've learnt that if I don't take any action little or nothing will change. If you don't want change and are happy with your life when you are being honest with yourself that's great. Again, I realised that I can't complain about the consequences of my actions if I'm not prepared to change anything. I'm sure you may well know someone that complains about the same situation, person or problem time after time and wonder why things aren't different. Knowing that our lives can be better is a great motivation, if others can achieve it so can we.

As Albert Einstein once said, "The definition of insanity is doing the same thing repeatedly and expecting different results".

Its hard work to change but it is possible, and I'm living proof of that. I do appreciate some people just want to cope and manage with their lives instead of changing, that wasn't a choice I was willing to settle for. I recently saw an article about an MP called Liam Byrne who had spoken out about his personal experience of living with an alcoholic father. I was so moved that he had shared his story publicly that I wanted to contact him. So, I emailed him and he responded - it was great to share experiences.

Some months later he invited me to an event at the House of Commons, linked to a charity called National Association of Children of Alcoholics (NACOA). I was amazed by the number of people in the room that were just like me; the adult children of alcoholics. Some of them were still living with it; and some no longer had it in their lives but were still affected. I took Mum with me and it was a very moving few hours, I felt that this charity was doing good by helping those like me.

Sometime later I decided to email NACOA and offered to help - they had several positions but most were too far away from where I live. They did however have a media role; to go into schools and talk at assemblies about NACOA, how they help people living with a parent's drinking.

After a short while I attended a training course and I'm now able to start supporting them. This feels great and I know the work will be fulfilling. I met other people just like me whilst training and hearing their stories was heart-warming and heart-breaking at the same time.

I can't wait to get started and start delivering the talks in local schools. You never know where things go but I'm excited for the future and what it may hold. I just hope that having the MP's involvement will help to raise the awareness of this awful illness, and how it affects the family.

For example, my sister Daisy has suffered from alcohol misuse for a few years. This is something that I find difficult, for obvious reasons; there have been so many similarities to my Dad. I was there to support her through her first detox; but unfortunately, it didn't work and I've had to take a step back because I find it too painful to deal with. I have told my oldest nephew about NACOA so he has someone outside the family he can call if he needs to.

Daisy is unfortunately going down the same road as our Dad; I do have a lot of empathy for her as I understand why she has taken this route. We have to allow her the dignity to sort out her own life; something I learnt from my Al-Anon meetings.

> **Fact**
>
> **The NIAAA say that alcoholism is a disease. The craving that an alcoholic feel for alcohol can be as strong as the need for food or water. An alcoholic will continue to drink despite serious family, health or legal problems.**

Unfortunately, she has two sons, and I'm aware (as is my Mum and their dad) that they're in the same situation that we lived through as children.

From my experience and learning I must protect myself so that I look after my own wellbeing. There's no point being involved if I just make matters worse.

She is my sister and I love her of course, but sometimes you don't like people's behaviour. I hope with all my heart that she finds her way to sobriety and she can keep away from the drink for her children and herself. It breaks my heart to see this happening to my own sister but I accept this is the road she is on. She is doing well at the moment and the changes she is making are positive. She deserves to have her life back again and to be happy .

Chapter 37 - Wow

My journey of self-discovery started when I was just 21 years old. I'm 41 years old now, and I know that it will be something I do for the rest of my life. Once you start on this journey you know it will be ongoing, it is a way of life.

For several years, I was still finding my feet although I became more educated and aware with each step I took. It's only now that I feel I've finally reached a place where I feel content and have more acceptance of myself.

This has not been an easy process; and my being single for the past seven years has been difficult at times. Not because I don't enjoy my own company now, but because I believe life is to be shared and I want to share my experiences with someone.

Now is the time for me to be with someone I connect with and trust; someone who will put me first. That may sound selfish but I feel that throughout my life I haven't been anyone's priority apart from in one of my relationships. I felt Mark put me first and knew me and took time to get to know everything about me and what was important to me, which was the best feeling in the world. It was a novelty because it wasn't a feeling I had experienced before; sadly, at the time I didn't appreciate it.

Through these past seven years of being single I've learnt so much about myself. I know I need to be myself and not pretend - if someone doesn't like a confident person with strong conviction then I'm not the one for them. That is true for friendships as well as personal relationships.

I remember analysing myself and thinking that I had to change everything I didn't like. It is only in the past few years that I've come to understand that I want to just be me. One person may see my confidence and opinions as a positive thing; so, it isn't an issue - why change that? Of course, I could flip between one personality and another, that is exactly what I had been doing. No more!

Relationships have begun to improve and I accept myself more. As time progresses I see therapists less and now I only see a Kinesiologist. She is amazing and I trust her whole-heartedly. I see her monthly as this is like a regular health check for me.

She works with the body to release negative energies and realign things. I don't fully understand how it works but I don't need to know. I have developed a trust in others and know that I don't have to know everything all the time.

This was certainly something that was difficult to develop as a child of an alcoholic; we like control and letting go was something I have struggled with my whole life. In certain contexts, I'm now able to trust that things will be OK. I no longer need to know the end goal or where things are headed all the time. I can just wait to see what happens.

So, what now? Well now my life is in a place of change and

I'm embracing the change the only way I know how, full on. I'm doing all I can to promote and develop my business and I'm hoping that this year is the year I find the man of my dreams.

My Facebook group called 'Change your Mind' supports children of alcoholics and those affected by someone's drinking that want the support they may not have ever had, to feel connected and be with other likeminded people. Although we learnt from a young age to keep it all quiet, if anything is going to change in ourselves as well as in the wider world, then we *must* talk about it, we have nothing to be ashamed about.

For me, I will continue my mission to raise awareness about the impact of alcohol on others, be a good friend and keep growing. I will keep on learning and developing and be as authentic as I can be. I've come such a long way, learnt so much, put to bed so many issues and bad experiences; and have more resilience now than ever.

Today I'm better able to cope with the trials and tribulations of life - I know that it can never be plain sailing, but that is part of the tapestry of life. Without those challenges, we can't learn and we can't appreciate what we have.

I will continue attracting the right people into my life and letting the wrong ones go. Most of all I want to have fun, laugh and live life to the full.

You can find more information about me on my website www.johuey.co.uk or visit my Facebook page www.facebook.com/jolhuey

My Recommended Resources

Louise Hay – www.louisehay.com

Susan Jeffers – www.susanjeffers.com

Mindfulness Meditation – Look for anything by Jon Kabat-Zinn

Emotional Freedom Technique – www.emofree.com

National Association of Children Of Alcoholics (NACOA) – www.nacoa.org.uk

Al-anon - http://www.al-anonuk.org.uk

Drug Fam – http://www.drugfam.co.uk

The laundry list - http://www.adultchildren.org/lit-Laundry_List

Adult Children of Alcoholics - http://www.adultchildren.org

Richard Bandler - http://richardbandler.com

The Samaritans - http://www.samaritans.org

Bottled Up – www.bottled-up.com

Book Recommendations

I'm OK You're OK by Thomas A. Harris

Staying OK by Amy B Harris and Thomas A. Harris

Women Who Love Too Much by Robin Norwood

Women Who Think Too Much by Nolen-Hoeksema

Perfect Daughters by Robert Ackerman

The Games People Play by Eric Byrne

The Monk Who Sold His Ferrari by Robin Sharma

Adult Children of Alcoholics by Janet G. Woititz

Healing the Child Within by Charles L. Whitfield

A Gift to Myself Personal Workbook and guide by Charles L.Whitfield

The Chimp Paradox by Prof Steve Peters

Reinventing your Life by Jeffrey E Young

Interesting Facts

- More than 9 million people in England drink more than the recommended daily limits

NHS, 2012 ' Social Drinking' The Hidden Risks

- A research study with 4,000 respondents estimates there are 3 million children in the UK living with parental alcohol problems

- Alcohol related harm costs England around £21bn per year, with £3.5bn to the NHS, £11bn tackling alcohol-related crime and £7.3bn from lost work days and productivity costs

   House of Commons Health Committee, 2012, Government's Alcohol Strategy

- For every £1 invested in specialist alcohol treatment, £5 is saved on health, welfare and crime costs

   Raistrick, D Heather, N Godfry, C (2006) Review of the effectiveness of treatment for alcohol problems London: National Treatment Agency of Substance Misuse

- Almost half of young people excluded from school in the UK are regular drinkers

   Ibid

- Recommended weekly allowance from NHS – 14 units per week

- It takes on average 1 hour to digest 1 unit of alcohol

- 10% of all dementia cases are related to alcohol consumption which makes it the 2nd leading cause of dementia

- Elder people tend to drink more frequently than younger people. The proportion of adults who drank every day increased with each group – just 1% of 16-25 year olds had drunk every day during the previous week, 4% of 25-44's, 9% of 25-64's and 13% of 65+

General Lifestyle Survey, 2011

- The World Health Organisation estimates that there are 140 million people with alcoholism or alcohol dependence syndrome worldwide

- In the UK, the NHS breaks down 'alcohol misuse' into the following three categories - hazardous, harmful and dependent drinking

- A complex mixture of genetic and environmental factors influences the risk of the development of alcoholism

How I can support you

If you are open and committed and want to see some changes in your life then Jo has a number of options available on her website.

Jo's offers an online programme to understand more about fear, loneliness, feelings, anxiety and feeling overwhelmed. You'll learn new techniques, tips and practical ways to make changes to suit you.

If you'd like to receive honest tried and tested self-help content by email you can sign up for Jo's weekly news here:
http://bit.ly/JHInsights

www.johuey.co.uk

Acknowledgments

I'd like to say thank you to my family and friends who've seen me grow and change over the years. They've supported me when I've been low, and patiently listened without judgement. I appreciate their loyalty and acceptance.

I'd like to thank my friends at the Dorset NLP Forum who've made me feel welcome and safe; this has been a key part of the positive life changes I'm now experiencing.

I'd also like to pay tribute to Al-Anon, which gave me the connection to other like-minded people I'd been searching for my whole life. Joining Al-Anon was a turning point for me.

Also, a big thank you to Laura who has been such an amazing support with writing this book and a true friend. She's been the objective voice I need but with kindness and expertise to get my book to print. Also thank you to Allegra for being a third eye on this book and Katrina for designing my amazing cover.

Lastly a big thank you to all my readers, I hope you found the book insightful and helpful.

I did it!!!

Whatever you seek you can do it too.